RAND

Resources, Costs, and Efficiency of Training in the Total Army School System

Michael G. Shanley, John D. Winkler, Paul S. Steinberg

Prepared for the
United States Army

Arroyo Center

Preface

The U.S. Army has launched a series of initiatives to streamline and consolidate its extensive system of schools, covering training institutions that serve both active and reserve forces. Prominent among these initiatives is a prototype regional school system the Army established in the southeastern region of the United States during fiscal years (FY) 1994 and 1995, which fundamentally changed the organization and management of Reserve Component (RC) training institutions run by the Army National Guard (ARNG) and the U.S. Army Reserve (USAR). The objectives of this initiative were to achieve economies and ensure the quality of training, while laying the foundation for a "Total Army School System" (TASS) that would be more efficient and integrated across the Active Component (AC) and the Army's two Reserve Components (RC).

As this reorganization got under way, RAND's Arroyo Center was asked to provide an objective assessment of the performance and efficiency of its system of schools, including the regional prototype. This report presents final results for one of the major areas in the assessment, which examined resource use and efficiency both inside and outside the prototype during FY95 (the execution year) of training. A forthcoming RAND report on "Managing Training Requirements and School Production in the Total Army School System" examines the school system's ability to meet training requirements, while a third forthcoming report on "Performance and Efficiency of the Total Army School System" provides an overall summary of RAND's final results.

The research was sponsored by the Deputy Commanding General, U.S. Army Training and Doctrine Command, and was conducted in the Arroyo Center's Manpower and Training Program. The Arroyo Center is a federally funded research and development center sponsored by the United States Army.

Contents

vi

Figures

Tables

Summary

Introduction

This report analyzes the resource use and efficiency of the new prototype school system established by the Reserve Components (RC) in the southeast section of the United States (Region C). The assessment of outcomes in FY95 (the execution year of the prototype) is based on data collected in both FY94 (the baseline year) and FY95 in Region C and Region E, a comparison region in the midwest. The document also discusses ways to further improve resource use and efficiency in the future—primarily by more fully utilizing school system capacity. Because the school system is currently falling far short of meeting RC training demand, we focus on more effectively using current school resources rather than on achieving manpower or dollar savings. However, if training requirements decrease in the future, the results of this research could be applied to achieve resource savings. This report is part of a larger effort by RAND's Arroyo Center to analyze the performance and efficiency of the RC school system.

Resources and Costs of Training in RC Schools

In FY95 (as was the case in FY94), the cost of training in RC schools in Regions C and E was slightly more than $80 million. Manpower resources—school manpower and student days—account for most of that total, about 87 percent. Travel costs represent only about 7 percent of total costs in FY95, but could increase and become an issue in the future if the school system is further consolidated.

Given that the RC school system needs to train substantially more soldiers than it did in FY95 to accommodate the total requirement, increased efficiency in the school system will mean greater student production and improved utilization of the school's key resource—manpower—rather than achieving dollar savings. In fact, dollar savings would not be large even if the school system were scaled back. Over 80 percent of the total cost of RC training was funded out of the normal 38- or 39-day training schedule of RC soldiers, with the remaining 19 percent representing supplemental dollar funding earmarked for RC training. Thus, we found relatively little dollar funding that could be cut back.

FY95 Efficiency of Training in RC Schools

During FY95, the prototype in Region C implemented considerable consolidation and specialization. For example, the new school system reduced the number of school administrative organizations by 35 percent; courses taught in the Annual Training (AT) mode are being focused at fewer locations (41 percent fewer locations, with 30 percent more classes taught per location), without making students travel farther distances to get there; and with the increased specialization, the number of career management fields (CMFs) a school has to support has decreased more than 50 percent. We believe that such changes have set the stage for efficiency gains in the future.

However, despite these trends, Region C efficiency decreased somewhat in FY95. Using our primary measure of efficiency—school mandays per 100 student days—we estimated that it took 62 days of instructor and staff support to produce 100 days of student training in FY94. In FY95, the number of instructor and staff support days needed increased to 67 per 100—a decrease in efficiency of about 8 percent.

Still, when we examine this result in more detail, we find that the decrease in Region C efficiency reflects transitional issues associated with the implementation of the prototype, not fundamental problems with the prototype design itself. The transitional issues include a wait for the scheduled implementation of the U.S. Army Reserves (USAR) reduction in staff manpower, a major transition in instructors and operating procedures for most school organizations, and a decline in enrollments for noncommissioned officer education system (NCOES) courses.

Increasing Efficiency Through Improved Capacity Use

We conclude that significant future efficiency gains are possible in Region C—and, by extension, in other RC school organizations—by more effectively using school system capacity. Using a model of operational manpower in the schools, we examined potential improvement in school mandays per 100 student days from employing three strategies: (1) implementing the planned consolidation in the USAR of Table of Distribution and Allowances (TDA) staff; (2) increasing student throughput to gain scale economies; and (3) improving the match of instructors to student inputs to achieve a more optimal mix. After calculating the effect of each strategy independently (to give an idea of their relative effectiveness), we then calculated the combined effect of employing all three simultaneously.

Using the Combat Service Support (CSS) Brigade as an example,[1] we find that the first strategy of reducing the number of personnel required in TDA staff positions will lead to an efficiency gain of about 12 percent—from the current 59 school mandays needed for each 100 student days of output to 52. This assumes that student load remains the same and that the reduced staff can supply adequate support within the new school organization. Employing strategy 2 in the CSS Brigade—increasing student throughput—yields an efficiency improvement of 10 percent—from 59 to 53—when student load is increased by 50 percent (the level implied by FY95 allocations). The improvement from employing strategy 3—optimally utilizing all FY95 instructors—yields the largest efficiency improvement—17 percent in the CSS brigade, from 59 to 49.

Employing all three strategies together yields greater efficiency gains than using any one strategy by itself. For example, suppose the CSS Brigade had been able to train the increased student load specified in FY95 allocations, while using the reduced staff specified in the November FY95 TDA. This would imply a considerable improvement in the match of instructors to students, since underutilized instructors usually resulted from low fill rates and canceled classes. In this case, efficiency would improve 24 percent—from 59 to 45. In other brigades, we conclude that potential improvements in efficiency would be similar.

Increasing Efficiency Through Further Consolidation

As mentioned, the new Region C school system has already reduced the number of AT training locations by 41 percent. Moreover, another effort by the Army National Guard (ARNG) is taking place nationwide to create "superregional" sites for training in specific career fields. While fewer training sites can translate into a reduction in required support manpower, it also means higher travel costs for students who have to travel greater distances to reach those sites. The question is, how many locations for particular types of courses are ideal?

Our analysis shows that having less than one AT training location per region for a course (the so-called superregional training sites) is efficient when support costs are high, such as they are for Combat Arms (CA) courses. For example, in the case of the 11M AT, our data suggest that four sites (as opposed to the current six sites) would be optimal, yielding a 7 percent savings in the training of that military occupational specialty (MOS).

---

[1]The USAR CSS Brigade is used as an example, but without including the RTS-Ms that are operated by the ARNG.

For Inactive Duty Training (IDT), the questions are similar, but the focus changes from a national to a local one. Can the number of IDT weekend training sites be productively reduced without unreasonably increasing the cost of travel? We found that for the typical IDT course in the present environment (which does not include distance learning), the data did not support further training site consolidation.

Recommendations

The results of our assessment indicate that efficiency can improve in the RC school system, providing appropriate changes can be implemented. Based on our analysis, we recommend that steps be taken to bring more soldiers to RC schools and to improve the match between instructors and students to achieve larger class sizes and more fully utilize available instructors. The match between instructors and students will get better if predictions of student inputs can be made more accurate, if better information can be provided to schools for hiring instructors, and if the student manpower system (including the school TDA structure) can be made more flexible in responding to unpredicted changes in demand. This can be done, for example, by continuously adjusting school TDAs to match changing requirements and by increasing the accessibility of trained part-time instructors (e.g., through a national instructor registry). To a lesser extent, we also see improvements in efficiency from regionalizing ATs for high-support courses. Finally, to support future improvements in efficiency, we see the need for sufficient supplemental resources to design more cost-effective work procedures to support the consolidation of training staffs, and we recommend developing a tracking system to monitor efficiency.

Acknowledgments

The authors benefited from support and assistance provided by many people in the U.S. Army. First, we owe particular thanks to our sponsors and successive Chairmen of the TASS General Officer Steering Committee: first Lieutenant General John E. Miller, Deputy Commanding General, U.S. Army Training and Doctrine Command (TRADOC), and then Lieutenant General Leonard D. Holder, Jr., Commanding General, U.S. Army Combined Arms Center. In addition, we are grateful for the support and assistance of the staff at the Army National Guard, First U.S. Army, the U.S. Army Reserve Command (USARC), and TRADOC's Office of the Deputy Chief of Staff for Training, including the TRADOC Coordinating Element (TCE) and Regional Coordinating Element (RCE) responsible for the Total Army School System (TASS). We also received key assistance from the staff of the State Adjutants General and Major U.S. Army Reserve Commands (MUSARCs) in the midwestern and southeastern United States—especially from the 108th Training Division of Charlotte, North Carolina and from the staffs and instructors in the many RC schools who bore the burden of data collection for this study. All provided access to data, information, and advice throughout the study, and they made it possible for us to observe training events and discuss training issues with staff, instructors, and students, all of which formed the basis of the analysis in this report. Finally, Major Robert James of the 108th Training Division made much of this report's analysis possible by helping us gain access to, and interpret data from, the USAR's DOLFINS data system.

We are also grateful for assistance received from our RAND colleagues. Useful comments on developing this research were provided by J. Michael Polich, Diane Green, and especially Jim Crowley, who also made numerous helpful suggestions on preliminary drafts. Invaluable computer support to effectively deal with a large number of diverse data files was provided by Rodger Madison and Laurie McDonald. Finally, Marilyn Yokota provided valuable research assistance, and Linda Daly, Jennifer Hawes-Dawson, Afshin Rastegar, and Eva Feldman designed and managed data collection and processing.

We have benefited greatly from assistance provided by all these sources. Errors of fact or interpretation, of course, remain the authors' responsibility.

Abbreviations

AC	Active Component
ADSW	Active Duty for Special Work
ADT	Active Duty for Training
AGR	Active Guard and Reserve
ANCOC	Advanced NCO Course
ARNG	U.S. Army National Guard
ASI	Additional Skill Identifier
AT	Annual Training
ATSC	Army Training Support Center
ATRRS	Army Training Requirements and Resources System
BNCOC	Basic NCO Course
CA	Combat Arms
CEAC	[Army's] Cost and Economic Analysis Center
CMF	Career management field
CONUSA	Continental United States Army
CS	Combat Support
CSS	Combat Service Support
DMOSQ	Duty MOS Qualified
FY	Fiscal Year
HS	Health Services
IDT	Inactive Duty Training
MDEP	Management Decision Package
MOS	Military Occupational Specialty
MTOE	Modified Table of Organization and Equipment
MUSARC	Major U.S. Army Reserve Command
NCO	Noncommissioned Officer

NCOA	NCO Academy
NCOES	NCO Education System
NGB	National Guard Bureau
O&M	Operations and Maintenance
O&S	Operations and Support
OES	Officer Education System
OPTEMPO	Operating Tempo
PLDC	Primary Leadership Development Course
POI	Program of Instruction
POL	Petroleum, Oil, and Lubricants
RC	Reserve Components
RCE	Regional Coordinating Element
RCTI	Reserve Component Training Institution
RTS	Regional Training Site
RTS-I	Regional Training Site-Intelligence
RTS-M	Regional Training Site-Maintenance
RTS-Med	Regional Training Site-Medical
SIDPERS	Standard Installation/Division Personnel System
SMA	State Military Academy
SQI	Skill Qualification Identifier
SSSC	Self-Service Supply Center
TAG	The Adjutant General
TASS	Total Army School System
TDA	Table of Distribution and Allowances
TDY	Temporary Duty
TOE	Table of Organization and Equipment
TRADOC	U.S. Army Training and Doctrine Command
USAR	U.S. Army Reserve
USARC	U.S. Army Reserve Command
USARF	U.S. Army Reserve Forces

1. Introduction

Background

For some time, the U.S. Army has recognized persistent problems in its extensive system of schools that provide technical and leadership training for the Reserve Components (RC), composed of the U.S. Army National Guard (ARNG) and the U.S. Army Reserve (USAR). Critics in recent years have suggested, for example, that the system lacks efficiency, provides inconsistent quality of training, and is difficult to manage to meet the training needs of RC units.[1] To respond to these concerns, the Army began (starting in FY94) a test of a "prototype" regional school system in the southeastern United States (Region C)—the states of North Carolina, South Carolina, Georgia, and Florida[2]—with the intention of broadening it nationwide after a suitable period of testing. The prototype embodied significant changes to the organization and management of training, and the intent was to raise standards and improve resource utilization. These changes were also aimed at achieving a longer-term goal—establishing a cohesive and efficient Total Army School System (TASS) of fully accredited and integrated schools to serve all Army components.

As these changes got under way, the Army asked RAND's Arroyo Center to analyze the operations of the system of schools serving the RC and assess whether the changes embodied in the prototype were improving the system's performance and efficiency. Initially, as the prototype school system was implemented (in FY94), RAND published a baseline assessment describing conditions and problems in RC schools in three areas: training requirements and school production, training resources and costs, and quality of training.[3] The intention was to provide a starting point for measuring changes and improvements in the system and the prototype, to be followed by a subsequent assessment after a year of execution (in FY95).

For part of the assessment, the Arroyo Center analyzed the performance and efficiency of the entire RC school system in relation to the prototype regional

---

[1]See, for example, Department of the Army Inspector General (1993).

[2]Region C also includes Puerto Rico and the Virgin Islands, but these locations were not included in the prototype.

[3]See Winkler et al. (1996) for a complete discussion of the baseline assessment.

school system (Region C). In other analyses, such as the one for resources and costs, Region C was compared with another region of the country, Region E, which includes Minnesota, Wisconsin, Illinois, Indiana, Ohio, Iowa,[4] and Michigan.

Objectives

This document focuses on resources and costs, analyzing resource use and efficiency in RC schools during FY95 (the execution year of the prototype), based on data collected in Regions C and E. It also offers ways to improve the efficiency of the school structures established in the prototype, primarily through improved use of capacity and further consolidation. We focus on efficiency improvement in terms of more effective use of current resources, as opposed to manpower and dollar savings, because the school system is currently falling far short of meeting the current training demand.[5] In other words, we see the benefits of improved efficiency in terms of increased RC readiness rather than resource reductions. Finally, the report discusses some broader policies needed to improve the system's overall efficiency and effectiveness.

Approach

In assessing training resources and costs in FY95, we used, in part, the same approach used in the FY94 analysis, which involved specifying quantifiable measures for the area. In this case, we identified the primary categories of resources needed by school organizations, determined the primary sources from which they were funded, and developed measures for comparing the relative efficiency and resource status of different school organizations. (These categories, sources, and measures are briefly described in Sections 2 and 3.)

To assess changes in efficiency from the prototype, we compared FY95 data with FY94 data in Region C, using the same comparison in Region E as a control for larger changes in the system. Finally, to address potential efficiency improvements in the future, we used the current student load and prototype school characteristics as a baseline and then established model parameters

---

[4]Iowa was included in the comparison region even though the state was reassigned to Region F near the end of the evaluation period.

[5]See the forthcoming companion document ("Managing Training Requirements and School Production in the Total Army School System"), which focuses on the analysis of training requirements and school production. It shows that current school quotas are less than half the training requirement for DMOSQ courses and less than two-thirds of the NCOES requirement.

(constructed from established Army plans and regulations and from special case studies conducted as part of this research) to examine alternative outcomes.

Data Sources

Because of the difficulty of using existing data to assess resources and costs, we had to develop new data-collection methods and instruments, as well as new data. To obtain measures of resource utilization and calculate training costs, we developed instruments that permitted standardization of data elements across various organizations and obtained cost factors and resource and funding data from national and regional RC commands, from RC schools, and from instructors and students at RC schools where we observed training. More specifically, the new data were collected from a subset of the school system—RC commands and RC schools in Region C and Region E—and a subset of sampled courses within that subset of RC schools. In FY94, we worked with 44 RC schools—18 and 26 schools in Regions C and E, respectively—broken down into four types:

- U.S. Army Reserve Forces (USARF) schools;
- State military academies (SMAs), managed by the ARNG and its state elements;
- NCO academies (NCOAs) in various areas of the country, belonging to both the USAR and ARNG;
- Regional training sites (RTS), covering the specific functional area of maintenance (RTS-M).

In FY95, we continued to work with the 26 RC schools in Region E. However, as a result of the school reorganization in Region C, the 18 RC schools were consolidated into 6 functionally aligned school brigades,[6] accompanied by a change in schools' missions from multifunctional to specialized. Each brigade, in turn, became the responsibility of a specific RC, with the USAR responsible for four brigades—Combat Support (CS), Combat Service Support (CSS), Officer Education, and Health Services (HS)—and the ARNG responsible for the Combat Arms (CA) and Leadership brigades. Moreover, the USAR transferred its schools' command and control from Army Reserve Commands to training divisions, which realigned training responsibilities under one umbrella consisting of both Initial Entry Training (IET) and schools' missions.

---

[6]*Concept Plan for Organizing a Total Army Training Structure (TATS) Individual Institutional Training System,* U.S. Army Training and Doctrine Command, 1993.

4

As in FY94, data in FY95 were collected from a number of sources:[7]

- Major USAR and ARNG commands—the U.S. Army Reserve Command (USARC) and the National Guard Bureau (NGB)—provided information on personnel cost factors, as well as school Tables of Distribution and Allowance (TDAs). In addition, the USARC provided access to data on reserve personnel pay and travel costs contained in the USAR's DOLFINS data system.

- The Adjutants General (TAGs) and Major U.S. Army Reserve Commands (MUSARCs) within Regions C and E provided financial data about the cost of (1) supporting schools in Regions C and E, and (2) sending students under their command to training, regardless of where attended.

- Reports from the Army Training Requirements and Resources System (ATRRS) provided information on student inputs and graduates for each class of each school (with corrections and updates provided by the RC schools); these data enabled us to compute student days.

- The RC schools in the two regions filled out administrative reports that provided information about the number of full- and part-time military personnel and civilian personnel actually working at the school during FY95. In addition, RC schools provided information about the number and type of borrowed and paid-for mandays supporting the school, as well as information about the location of training.

- The RC schools involved with the sampled courses provided data in four areas:

  - A student form that listed all students enrolled in the course by grade, component, pay status, and distance traveled to training;
  - A school manpower form that provided the same information for instructor and school staff manpower and added information about the source of the manning (from the school or another unit), the function of each person in supporting training (e.g., instructor, operations, administration, logistics), and the number of courses the person supported;
  - An equipment form that listed all Class VII equipment used in the course, along with the operating tempo (OPTEMPO) and source of that equipment; and
  - A financial form that listed all supplies and materials, contracts, and leases involved with conducting the course.

---

[7]See Winkler et al. (1996) for a more detailed discussion of the data sources.

- We visited 15 RC schools and administered questionnaires to students and instructors (531 student questionnaires and 611 instructor questionnaires within 50 sampled courses) to collect information about unreimbursed travel expenses and to verify the pay status of students. We also asked about pay status for students during the Inactive Duty Training (IDT) phase of their training.

- Other sources included the Army Training Support Center (ATSC), which provided information on the duplication and distribution of courseware, and 1st U.S. Army, which supplied instructor and staff assignments for Region E. In addition, personnel and equipment OPTEMPO-based factors were provided by the Army's Cost and Economic Analysis Center (CEAC).

These data were used as the basis for measuring efficiency inside and outside the prototype and served as the inputs into the modeling done to measure the potential effects on efficiency of improving capacity and further consolidation within Region C.

Organization of This Report

In the next section we examine the costs and resource drivers involved in RC schools training in FY95. Section 3 examines efficiency in RC schools training in FY95. Sections 4 and 5 examine ways to improve efficiency in the prototype through improved capacity use and through further consolidation, respectively. Section 6 presents our recommendations.

The appendix explains the process of tracking resources and costs.

2. Resources and Costs of Training in RC Schools

In this section we examine the question of what resources and costs drive the operation of the RC school system. In particular, we define total operations cost, examine the resource areas and funding sources that make up total operations cost, and assess how those cost drivers operated in FY95. In addition, we focus on the issue of travel costs as a percentage of total costs—a pertinent issue in FY95 with the initiation of the more consolidated school system in Region C.

Costs, Resource Areas, and Funding Sources

In the analysis for both FY94 and FY95, we sought to capture the total cost of the RC training system below the level of "higher-level support." Thus, we included the recorded costs of training delivery, the cost of borrowed manpower and supplies (often expended on borrowed equipment), the cost of student pay and temporary duty (TDY) while attending training, and the cost of installation support.[1] Not included in total operations cost are higher-level support costs, including the cost of courseware development, the cost of school accreditation and assistance borne by U.S. Army Training and Doctrine Command (TRADOC) Headquarters and proponent schools, and the cost of school coordination and management borne by TAGs, MUSARCs, Continental United States Armies (CONUSAs), the Regional Coordinating Element (RCE), and the Title XI program. The costs considered are described under four "resource areas" below. Together, the cost of these resources represents a large percentage of the total cost of the system and that part most pertinent to the concerns addressed in this study.

As in the FY94 report, included costs are represented under four resource areas:

- **School staff.** This includes the military and civilian pay and allowances of RC school instructors and support staff, retirement accrual associated with

---

[1]Supply and installation costs do not include those for selected items of indirect support to training, including the cost of depot maintenance and medical support.

the pay, travel costs to the training site,[2] and (when allowed) per-diem costs associated with travel.[3]

- **Students**. This includes the pay and allowances of students while attending a course, the retirement accrual associated with the pay, travel costs to the training site, and (when allowed) per-diem costs associated with travel.

- **Mission operations and support**. This includes supplies and materials associated with the implementation of training—some in the OPTEMPO area (e.g., petroleum, oil, and lubricants (POL), maintenance, and repair parts), others in the non-OPTEMPO area (e.g., self-service supply center, SSSC); TDY resources associated with schools; contracts and leases associated with training (except those having to do with installation support, which are included in the fourth resource area); ammunition used in training exercises; and the resources used in courseware reproduction and distribution.

- **Installation support**. This includes the resource requirements of facilities (both manpower authorizations and budget dollars), covering both base operations and real property maintenance activities.

We also identified three broad "funding sources"[4] associated with the resource areas. In broad terms, training was funded, first, out of TDA spaces dedicated to schools (that might otherwise have been used to increase Table of Organization and Equipment (TOE) force structure). Second, training was funded out of discretionary dollars in the budget earmarked for that purpose. Third, training was funded out of personnel time and dollars originally earmarked for unit training, but donated by those units for the purposes of individual training. A detailed definition of each category follows.

- **TDA authorizations**. Most Army personnel costs derive from the funding of established Modified Table of Organization and Equipment (MTOE) or TDA manning structures that distribute Army end strength to particular Army units. RC schools have a TDA structure that includes the specification of a

---

[2]A small amount of travel costs to training sites, particularly to IDT training sites, is included under TDY, which we included under the "Mission operations and support" area.

[3]Note that the cost of military and civilian manpower is typically separated in the Department of Defense budgeting system. In the budgeting system, the cost of military personnel is included under the personnel appropriation, while the cost of civilians is included under the operations and maintenance appropriation.

[4]In the FY94 report, we had a fourth category of funding, "personal time," defined as the extra, unpaid days contributed by RCTI TDA staff. We did not feel we had accurate enough data to include that category in FY95.

8

given number of authorizations. We include the normal[5] pay and allowances[6] of such personnel under "TDA authorizations."

- **Supplemental dollars**. Supplemental dollars derive from discretionary funding sources that fund any student or school manpower days that represent additional training periods for soldiers (beyond their 39-day commitment), as well as the installation support and normal supplies and materials required to support those days. The Army accounting system categorizes the personnel portion of these costs as Active Duty for Training (ADT) student support and either ADT or Active Duty for Special Work (ADSW) staff support to schools. These are discretionary budgeted dollars in that they are a matter of individual TAG and MUSARC funding policy and not fixed by the decision of a component's end strength.

- **Unit AT/IDT**. When nonschool military personnel contribute part of their Annual Training (AT) or IDT training periods to the support of schools (we call these "borrowed mandays"), we say that those days, as well as the installation support and normal supplies and materials required to support them, are funded out of "unit training dollars." The term derives from three assumptions: (1) all authorized soldiers train a normal 39 days per year (or 260 for full-time Active Guard and Reserves (AGRs)); (2) the cost of those days, as well as the support those soldiers receive while training on those days, is sunk once end strength is determined (and for the purposes of this analysis); and (3) the default use of those days is for unit training.

Manpower Resources Dominate Cost

Figure 2.1 shows the total costs of training in Regions C and E for FY95, an amount that totaled $81.2 million.[7] As the figure plainly shows, manpower resources (the top two bars, showing school staff and students) dominate the cost of training in RC schools, accounting for 87 percent of the total. In addition, as shown by the divisions within the bars, a substantial portion of school training is funded with unit training dollars in that training is accomplished within the context of the 38- or 39-day-per-year training allotment associated with all Army authorized end strength. Supplemental dollars—that is, extra funding

---

[5]"Normal" means the pay and allowances for IDT and AT training. We do not include here any extra pay personnel receive for working extra duty.

[6]We include both the military pay and allowances of TDA personnel, and for those who are also "military technicians," we include their civilian pay and allowances.

[7]We found that the total cost for FY95 and the distribution of that cost by funding source and resource category were quite similar to those for FY94. The only exception worth mentioning concerns ADT/ADSW funds available to school staff, which decreased slightly in Region E and increased in Region C. See Winkler et al. (1996) for a full description of FY94 costs.

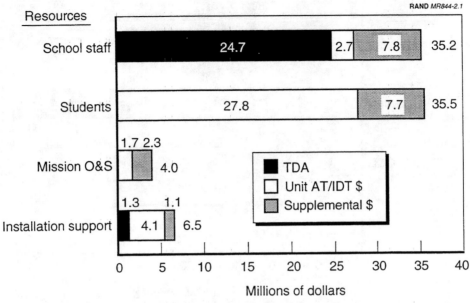

SOURCE: TAG/MUSARC administrative reports and RC schools survey.

Figure 2.1—Manpower Resources Drive the Total Cost of RC School Training

earmarked to augment training in RC schools—contributes relatively little to
total cost of training—overall, about 19 cents on the dollar.

Travel Costs Are a Small Portion of Total Costs

The regionalization and functional alignment of RC schools carried out in
implementing the prototype increased the geographic area for which a school is
responsible. Given concerns about the resulting widening span of control, we
specifically focused in this year's analysis on the issue of travel costs as a part of
the cost of training.

As Figure 2.2 shows, travel costs (the black part of the bars) in general account
for a small fraction of the total training cost in FY95, amounting to about 7
percent ($6 million out of the total $81 million) for those attending Region C and
E courses.[8]

---

[8]In fact, the 7 percent figure derived from Figure 2.2 actually represents an upper-bound
estimate of travel cost paid by the Army. While we have defined travel costs as the cost of both travel
and per diem, in practice some of the per-diem costs are incurred at the training site during the
course rather than in traveling to or from the training site.

10

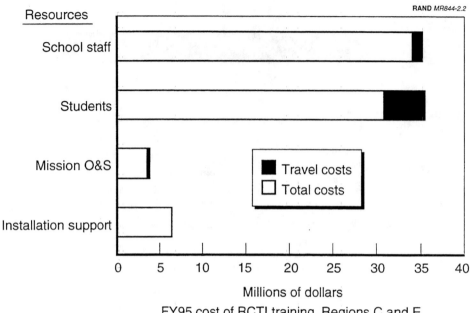

Figure 2.2—Travel Costs Are a Small Percentage of Total Costs

Thus, despite the consolidation of school organizations and functional alignment that occurred in Region C during this time, travel costs do not have much effect on costs or efficiency in the new school system. In essence, it turns out that between FY94 and FY95, the distances students traveled remained about the same. Specifically, students averaged about 370 miles travel to get to AT in FY95, a distance that is virtually identical to the FY94 figure. The distance students traveled to IDT training averaged 63 miles for Region C students in FY95, about 14 miles more on average than in FY94. However, whatever is driving that increase appears unrelated to the prototype, since nearly the same increase in distance occurred in Region E. Further, the extra distance does not translate into a significant increase in cost for the majority of students.

The implication of these findings is that for purposes of evaluating the new school system during its first year of operation, manpower resources are still the driving factor. As a result, we will continue to measure efficiency in the school system in FY95 using the same metric we used in FY94—comparing trained student days with the number of school mandays it took to produce that output. However, before turning to that discussion in Section 3, we first examine the travel data in a more disaggregated form.

Travel Costs Vary Between Students and Instructors

Table 2.1 shows the relative importance of per-diem costs for USAR[9] students and instructors traveling to AT. Total travel costs average $237 per AT for students and $168 for instructors. Of that total, nearly all for students and more than half for instructors goes toward airline tickets, private auto mileage, or the costs of other modes of transportation. Per-diem costs, contributing primarily to nonmilitary lodging and meals expenses, comprise about 16 percent of total travel costs for students and 45 percent of the total for instructors. Most of the costs for lodging and meals will presumably be incurred by students traveling long distances to training and, as such, are properly included with travel costs. However, some unknown amount of these costs is required during the training period; as a result, the total costs listed overestimate true travel costs.

Table 2.1 reveals additional details about costs paid by the USAR to send students to AT. First, AT travel costs are higher for students than for instructors. Students cost more because they travel longer distances than instructors on average and because they are typically traveling individually. Second, total travel costs for both students and instructors represent a considerably higher percentage of pay (22 and 10 percent, respectively) than the 7 percent amount shown in Figure 2.2.[10] The primary reason is that virtually all student travel costs are incurred during the AT periods. Figure 2.2 showed a lower figure because it also included the cost of weekend training (IDT), where almost no travel costs are paid.

Table 2.1

Travel Costs to Attend RC School Training in AT Mode

Average Cost	Paid to USAR Soldiers from Region C ($)	
	Students	Instructors
Total pay during course[a]	1,091	1,602
Travel costs	237	168
Privately owned vehicle (POV), airfare, etc.	199	92
Per diem	38	76
Travel costs as percent of total	22%	10%

SOURCE: 1994 DOLFINS.

[a]Includes pay, allowances, and travel costs. Travel periods of 8–19 days are included.

---

[9]Data in this detail were not available for students and instructors in the ARNG.

[10]Of course, as the distance traveled to AT increases, travel costs become an even higher proportion of total costs. For example, we found that in California, travel costs for USAR students traveling to AT were $360 on average, 50 percent higher than the cost for Region C students. In that case, the proportion of travel cost to total cost also went up from 22 to 29 percent.

Although Figure 2.2 and Table 2.1 show the cost of travel paid by the military, they do not consider the costs paid out of pocket by the soldiers themselves. According to survey reports from USAR instructors,[11] only about three-fifths of AT travel costs and as little as 5 percent of IDT travel costs were reimbursed by the Army. Per instructor, about $600 per person was paid out of pocket for FY95.[12] However, these costs were highly skewed toward those instructors paying the most out of pocket. While most instructors paid relatively modest amounts, in the highest quartile of expenses, Region C instructors paid an average of $1,200 in FY95 in unreimbursed travel costs. This, by the way, was not unique to instructors in Region C; similar, though only slightly lower, figures held true for USAR instructors in Region E.[13]

In summary, in FY95 (as in FY94), the cost of training in RC schools in Regions C and E was dominated by manpower costs, accounting for 87 percent of total costs. Moreover, travel costs represented about 7 percent of total costs in FY95. Given these findings, and given the fact that the RC school system needs to train substantially more soldiers than it did in FY95 to accommodate the total requirement, we conclude that increased efficiency in the school system will mean greater student production and improved utilization of the school's key resource—manpower—rather than dollar savings. In fact, dollar savings would not be large even if the school system were scaled back. Over 80 percent of the total cost of RC training was funded out of the normal 38- or 39-day training schedule of RC soldiers, with the remaining 19 percent representing supplemental dollar funding earmarked for RC training. Thus, we found little dollar funding that could be cut back.

---

[11]Costs for ARNG instructors were much less, because they tended to teach close to home base. In any case, we do not have enough information to quote a separate figure.

[12]Although we did not survey students to obtain a separate estimate, unreimbursed expenses appear to be less of a problem for them. On average, privately owned vehicle (POV) travel was paid 50 percent higher for students than for instructors.

[13]Some of the instructor-paid costs can be attributed to voluntary payments for POVs when a government vehicle was available or for a motel when government quarters were available, but most of them apparently resulted from unavoidable instructor travel costs that commands were unwilling or unable to reimburse. The increase in voluntary payments reflects declining travel budgets, the difficulty of matching an instructor to students for IDT training, and the dedication of many instructors to completing their mission. The fact that instructors bear these costs has a potentially important consequence: greater difficulties with instructor retention.

3. Efficiency of Training in RC Schools

In this section we examine how Region C and E fared in terms of efficiency in FY95. We begin by defining how we measure efficiency and identifying the factors that influence its value. We then compare the specific changes in efficiency over the two fiscal years (1994 and 1995) and discuss the significance of the changes observed.

How We Define Efficiency

To make judgments about efficiency, one must compare resource use (input) with the output produced. Since the results in Section 2 argue that manpower (both school staff and student) drives the total cost of training, it makes sense to compare those two resource areas in determining efficiency.[1] Thus, in our analysis we measure school efficiency by comparing school mandays to the student days they produce. The measure *we* choose—the ratio "school mandays per 100 student days"—is defined as all mandays used by the school (both instructor and staff, organic and nonorganic) divided by the number of student days produced. We further divided this measure into two parts—"instructor days per 100 student days" and "staff days per 100 student days." While these ratios are, in some ways, a cruder measure of efficiency than, for example, "total dollar costs per student," they have the advantage of relying on data that are much easier for the schools to collect if, as we recommend, such collection is made ongoing. Moreover, given the purpose of creating an ongoing monitoring system of school efficiency, we believe "school mandays per 100 student days" allows more meaningful comparisons than would a dollar cost measure.[2]

Five major factors have a large impact on the ratio of school mandays per 100 student days:

---

[1] We also judged that the data we received in the other two resource areas—"mission operations and support" and "installation support"—were of insufficient accuracy to make comparisons across RC components and school types.

[2] For example, one goal of a high-level monitoring system would be to compare the efficiency of the usage of school staff across school types. We do not want to assign a lower efficiency to NCOAs than to SMAs, for example, simply because the students and instructors are in a higher pay grade. We judged that issues of efficiency outside the scope of the measures we chose (such as the best manpower grade mix or civilian versus military mix) are of secondary importance to the monitoring system envisioned and, as such, should be addressed independently with supplemental data when they arise.

- **Training mission**—that portion of the training requirement the school is expected to conduct. More complex training missions specify smaller student-to-instructor ratios or require more mandays to provide training support, equipment, training devices, or facilities.

- **Specialization (or school design)**—the degree to which the school specializes in a subset of courses within a functional area versus the degree to which the school is multifunctional in design. If one assumes a fixed setup time to teach a course and common setup tasks for similar courses, the more a school can specialize, the less the fixed cost of preparation.

- **Size**—the number of classes (and training days) a school can conduct within a year. To the extent training demand can support them, larger schools can gain economies of scale because of the fixed support costs of setting up training.

- **Support arrangements**—how manpower, equipment, supplies, ammunition, and installation support are provided to the school. The more readily available these resources and the fewer and more established the contacts for obtaining them, the less effort required to coordinate their use for training.

- **Capacity utilization**—the degree to which schools can capitalize on the resources they have at their disposal to produce the maximum number of trained soldiers. Capacity is wasted when, for example, instructor-to-student ratios or instructor-to-support staff ratios are less than optimum or when courses are canceled or nonconducted.

Consolidation and Specialization Have Set the Stage for Efficiency Gains

During FY95, the prototype implementation in Region C included considerable consolidation and specialization. Figure 3.1 indicates the nature of these changes. Moving from the left of the figure, the new school system has reduced the number of schools by 35 percent. In addition, the courses taught in the AT mode are being focused at fewer locations (41 percent fewer locations, with 30 percent more classes taught per location), without making students travel farther distances to get there. Moreover, with the specialization, the number of career management fields (CMFs) a school has to support has decreased more than 50 percent.

In light of the factors that affect efficiency (listed above), one would expect the move toward consolidation and specialization in Region C to improve efficiency.

15

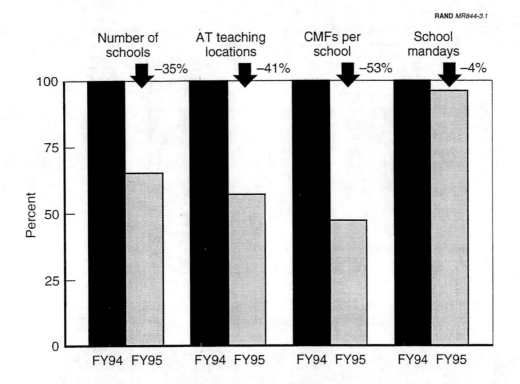

Figure 3.1—Consolidation and Specialization Are Setting the Stage for Efficiency Gains

However, efficiency gains should not necessarily be expected in FY95. We found that the schools are evolving toward more efficient combinations, setting the stage for efficiency gains in the future rather than realizing immediate gains. This conclusion is supported by the final set of bars in Figure 3.1, which shows that school mandays decreased by only 4 percent during FY95.

Region C Schools Became Slightly Less Efficient, While Region E Schools Became Slightly More

In fact, as shown in Figure 3.2—which compares the new Region C school system (in FY95) to its old one (in FY94) and to the Region E control region (in both FY94 and FY95)—Region C efficiency decreased somewhat in FY95.

In FY94, we estimated it took 62 days of instructor and staff support to produce 100 days of student training. In FY95, this fell by 8 percent, to 67 days per 100.

16

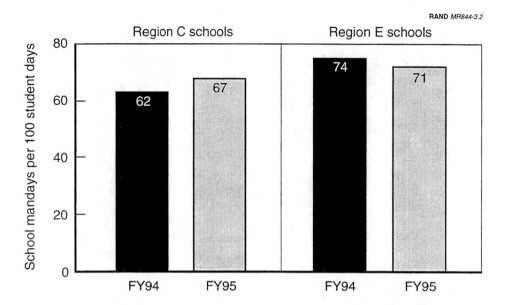

Figure 3.2—Change in Efficiency FY94 Versus FY95, Regions C and E

In contrast to Region C, efficiency in Region E improved slightly in FY95. In FY94, we estimated it took 74 days of instructor and staff support to produce 100 days of student training; in FY95, this improved by 4 percent, to 71 days per 100. However, even with the improvement in Region E and the slippage in Region C, Region C maintained the lower ratio among the two.[3]

Given the trends we saw in Figure 3.1, why do we see a decline in Region C efficiency in FY95? Is it a transitional effect in implementing the prototype, or does it reflect something more fundamentally problematic with the prototype structure itself?

The Decline in Efficiency Seems To Be a Transitional Issue

In fact, when we look at the data underlying the efficiency measurement— student load and school mandays—we see that the problem seems to reflect transitional problems during the implementation of the prototype, not fundamental problems with the prototype itself. The transitional issues include the wait for the scheduled reduction in school staff, a steep decline in student

---

[3]The lower ratio may result from a difference in course mix rather than a difference in RCTI practices. However, given the different school structures and missions, sorting out the course mix effect is beyond the scope of this report.

load, and a transition to a new instructor pool. These issues are further discussed below.

Table 3.1 displays the student load and school manpower data for both regions over the two fiscal years. The table shows, first, that student load decreased sharply in Region C, by 11 percent between the two fiscal years, while it increased by 5 percent in Region E. Second, during FY95, school manpower decreased in Region C (by 3 percent) and increased in Region E (by 2 percent). The potential effect of the USAR consolidation of manpower on efficiency could not be realized in Region C during the evaluation period because it was not scheduled to take place during FY95.[4] Thus, in Region C school manpower did not drop proportionally as much in the face of a significant drop in student load; in Region E, the increase in efficiency was driven by an increase in student days with a less than proportional (but not disproportional) increase in school mandays.

In both regions, the change in school manpower appeared to lag behind the change in student load. One potential explanation for the smaller change in training manpower is that a lag time is natural when reacting to change; that is, schools cannot fully adjust personnel levels during the same year that demand changes.

However, closer examination reveals more complex phenomena at work. Table 3.2 shows, for example, that instructor manpower in Region E increased (by 4 percent), a change nearly equal to the overall 5 percent increase in demand. However, in response to the 11 percent decrease in student load in Region C, both instructor and staff manpower decreased in Region C, but overall by only 3 percent, a much smaller amount.

Table 3.1

Changes in Student Load and School Manpower

Days	Region C			Region E		
	FY94	FY95	FY95/ FY94	FY94	FY95	FY95/ FY94
Student load	176,439	157,675	.89	204,599	215,664	1.05
School manpower	109,648	106,265	.97	151,655	154,186	1.02

SOURCE: ATRRS, RC schools survey, DOLFINS data from the USAR.

---

[4]The potential effect of the consolidation is addressed in Section 4.

What should we make of these changes? They need to be viewed in the context of the considerable turbulence brought about by the changes in the Region C school system. First, reducing support staff during a transition year proved especially difficult given the large number of special tasks generated by converting to the new school system. Second, large changes in TDAs required Region C USAR schools to transition from an established set of instructors to one that was substantially new while simultaneously accomplishing the traditional (and rapidly changing) training mission. This resulted in too many instructors in some courses, and not enough in others.[5]

Turbulence and need for adjustment was also created by how the student load declined. For example, when we disaggregate student load by training mode (as shown in Table 3.3), we see that the decline in weekend mode training was much steeper than the decline in AT mode training. This imbalance leads to a dilemma for schools regarding part-time instructors. If they keep enough instructors to cover AT training, they are faced with the problem of having instructors on the

Table 3.2

Changes in School Manpower

School Mandays	Region C			Region E		
	FY94	FY95	FY95/ FY94	FY94	FY95	FY95/ FY94
Instructor days	59,784	57,579	.96	75,305	78,085	1.04
Staff days	49,864	48,686	.98	76,350	76,101	1.00
Instructor/staff days	1.20	1.18	.98	.99	1.03	1.04
Total	109,648	106,265	.97	151,655	154,186	1.02

SOURCE: RC schools survey, DOLFINS data from the USAR.

Table 3.3

Changes in Student Load by Training Mode

Training Mode	Region C			Region E		
	FY94	FY95	FY95/ FY94	FY94	FY95	FY95/ FY94
Weekend mode (IDT)	48,595	36,245	.75	85,506	79,024	.92
AT mode	127,844	121,430	.95	119,093	136,640	1.15
Total	176,439	157,675	.89	204,599	215,664	1.05

SOURCE: RC schools survey, DOLFINS data from the USAR.

---

[5]See Section 4 for a fuller discussion of this issue.

weekends who are not teaching. On the other hand, if they reduce instructors to what is needed for weekend training, they create the need for either more borrowing of instructors to accomplish AT or the canceling of classes without instructors. In either case, staff workload is increased, and potential inefficiencies are introduced.

The nature of student load shifts can be understood more easily by examining the changes in student load by type of course. Table 3.4 shows that the regions look similar when we look at military occupational specialty qualification (MOSQ) courses—in both regions, we see a large increase in the duty military occupational specialty qualification (DMOSQ) student load, more than 15 percent. Similarly, both regions followed the national trend of decreased instruction in "other" courses—those outside the DMOSQ, Noncommissioned Officer Education System (NCOES), and Officer Education System (OES) arenas.[6]

The difference between the regions is largely focused on NCOES courses and on leadership courses in particular. In fact, nearly the entire decrease in Region C student load can be attributed to the decrease in Primary Leadership Development Course (PLDC) (which decreased by 24 percent) and Advanced NCO Course (ANCOC) and Basic NCO Course (BNCOC) courses taught in weekend mode (which decreased by 55 percent). Together, those changes resulted in an overall decrease of 25 percent in leadership courses in Region C, compared to only an 8 percent decrease in Region E.

Table 3.4

Changes in Student Load by Course Type

| Course Type | Region C | | | Region E | | |
	FY94	FY95	FY95/ FY94	FY94	FY95	FY95/ FY94
MOSQ	49,598	57,967	1.17	87,711	100,940	1.15
NCOES, II	11,995	9,604	.80	23,725	26,559	1.12
Leadership	69,797	52,367	.75	46,271	42,425	.92
Officer Education	14,653	13,736	.94	12,447	15,908	1.28
Other	30,399	25,003	.82	34,437	29,816	.87
Total	176,442	157,677	.89	204,591	215,648	1.05

SOURCE: ATRRS.

---

[6]Examples include OCS courses, SQI/ASI courses, and functional courses (e.g., NBC).

20

While such a shift may be appropriate given overtraining in NCOES,[7] at least some of the change in Region C can be attributed to organizational and administrative changes that substantially reduced the number of locations where leadership courses were available. Prior to FY95, a majority of RC schools across the country taught PLDC, ANCOC, and BNCOC at a large number of locations. While that practice continued in Region E in FY95, it began to change in Region C. For the four states there, all PLDC courses, as well as ANCOC and BNCOC courses taught in continuous mode, were taught at the Leadership Brigade in Leesburg, South Carolina. Further, the number of locations where ANCOC and BNCOC were taught in weekend mode decreased from 53 to 28 for BNCOC and from 31 to 17 for ANCOC.

In sum, the decrease in efficiency appears less related to underlying school system characteristics and more related to transitional issues, for example, a wait for the scheduled implementation of the USAR reduction in staff manpower, a major transition in instructors and operating procedures for most school organizations, and a steep decline in NCO enrollments.

Support Manpower Is the Driver of Efficiency Within Different RC School Organizations

So far, we have looked at changes in efficiency broadly between the two regions. But what do we learn when we look at the efficiencies of the various RC schools within the two regions? In this section, we examine efficiency in FY95 with respect to the different organizational structures in the two regions. Region E preserved the organizational structure that existed in both regions in FY94, while Region C transitioned to the new structure. Under both organizations, we confirmed that support manpower is a major driver of school efficiency.

Figure 3.3 compares the ratio of student mandays per 100 student days for the four traditional RC school organizational structures that existed in Region E during FY95. The two bars on the left represent specialized schools—the RTS-M specializes in wheeled-vehicle maintenance, and the NCOA specializes in leadership training. The two bars on the right represent multifunctional schools, the USARF schools in the USAR, and the SMAs in the ARNG.

As the figure shows, specialized school structures require less training manpower per student to support than the multifunctional schools. While

---

[7]See the forthcoming RAND report on "Managing Training Requirements and School Production in the Total Army School System."

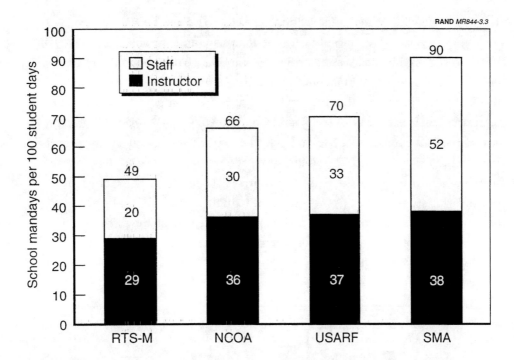

RAND MR844-3.3

Figure 3.3—School Mandays per 100 Student Days by Region E Organization

instructor manpower varies only slightly among the four types (the black part of
the columns), support (staff) manpower is less for the specialized schools.
Besides having the benefit of having to support fewer or a more homogeneous
set of courses, specialized schools also have the benefit of more consolidated
support on a fixed facility and a full-time staff. Multifunctional schools have to
coordinate training in a larger number of areas and for a wider range of courses
using primarily part-time military staff and borrowed equipment.

Figure 3.3 is similar to the comparable figure shown in our FY94 report that
covered both Regions C and E. The conclusions about traditional RC school
organizations—that specialized schools require less manpower to support than
multifunctional schools—are the same in FY95 as they were in FY94, but the
degree of difference between the two categories is less. In particular, the NCOA
appears to have required considerably more manpower per student in FY95 than
in FY94. We can trace the results here to a predicted (by quota allocations)
increase in student enrollments in NCO leadership courses that did not occur. In
effect, the NCOA found itself with excess manpower capacity (e.g., it had to use
lower than optimal student-instructor ratios) and not enough time to reallocate
that manpower to other uses.

22

Turning to new RC school organizations in Region C, Figure 3.4 shows the relative efficiencies (and the split between instructor and support manpower) of the new Region C brigades and verifies the importance of mission in explaining efficiency rates. In order of increasing manpower usage, the figure displays results for five brigades—Leadership, Combat Service Support (CSS), Combat Support (CS), Health Services (HS), and Combat Arms (CA)[8]—each of which covers the four-state area of Region C. At the low end of the scale, courses in the Leadership Brigade[9] used 52 training support days to produce 100 student days. At the other extreme, the CA Brigade required 121 training support days to produce 100 student days. As was the case with the former RC school organizations (as shown last year and this year in Region E), the primary driver of what makes one brigade more or less manpower-intensive than another is support (staff) manpower.

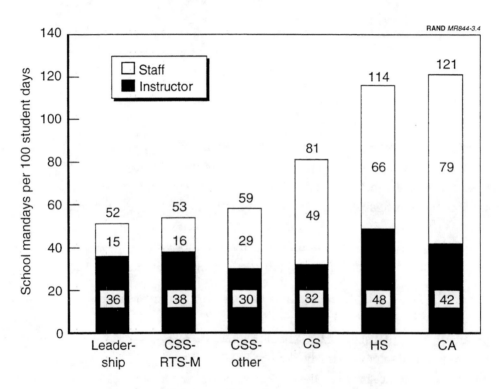

Figure 3.4—School Mandays per 100 Student Days by Region C Brigade

---

[8]The figures (school mandays and student days) for the "Combat Arms Brigade" include data relating to the General Studies Battalions in each state.

[9]School mandays and student days (the components of the efficiency measure) for the Leadership Brigade were constructed by adding to the figures from the Leesburg organization those from the former state academies (where weekend ANCOC and BNCOC courses were located in ATRRS), and those from the USAR detachment that provided instructors for ANCOC and BNCOC courses.

4. Increasing Efficiency Through Improved Capacity Use

Having established levels of efficiency of Region C schools in FY95, we now address potential ways to improve the region's capacity to produce trained students. After discussing the model used to analyze efficiency, this section focuses on three strategies for improving it: (1) consolidate TDA staff; (2) increase student throughput to gain scale economies; and (3) improve the match of instructors to student inputs to make it optimal. We examine each of these strategies individually to determine their potential for improving efficiency and then calculate the combined effect of employing all three simultaneously.

Modeling the Potential for Improving Capacity Use

To analyze efficiency, we first used FY95 Region C data as a baseline to model school mandays as a linear function of student load. Rather than constructing one generic model, we recognized the uniqueness of training in different functional areas by constructing a separate model for each Region C USAR brigade.[1] Although operational data from other parts of the country may produce models with substantially different parameters from those produced by the Region C data, we believe that the conclusions we draw from using the Region C models have much broader application.

To construct the model, we assumed that operating a school required a certain fixed number of staff to open, and then a variable number of instructors and staff whose size depended on the number of students attending. In equation form, the "total days" model for any brigade can be expressed as

$$y = a + bx \, ,$$

where y equals school mandays, a equals fixed staff mandays, b equals the ratio of variable school mandays to student days, and x equals student days.

---

[1]We focus here on USAR schools because their TDAs are the most firmly established. However, we believe the conclusions we draw from our analyses will also apply to ARNG schools.

Second, to examine efficiency at different student loads, we constructed an "efficiency" curve by simply dividing each side of the above equation by x, to achieve the following:

$$y/100x = b/100 + a/100x \, ,$$

where $y/100x$ equals school mandays per 100 student days, the measure of efficiency we discussed earlier in Section 3.

Finally, to examine the effect of employing alternative strategies to improve efficiency, we estimated the effect of those policies on the model's baseline parameters, a and b.

Below we explain the derivation of the baseline total days model, using the CSS Brigade in Region C for purposes of illustration.

Components of Manpower and Their Relationship to Student Load

We divided school mandays into three components to construct the model: (1) instructor mandays; (2) TDA staff mandays; and (3) supplemental staff days. Each of these is directly or indirectly a function of student load (i.e., teaching more students requires more training manpower), and each can be approximated by linear relationships (after some smoothing of "stepwise" relationships in the case of TDA staff mandays). Below, we explain the derivation of those relationships to construct the baseline model for each Region C USAR brigade.

Instructor mandays. Instructors are those personnel holding instructor positions on a school's TDA or those personnel borrowed from other units to teach a school course. Thus, instructor mandays refer to all those mandays worked by instructors for purposes of instruction, regardless of how funded.[2]

Actual FY95 instructor mandays used by each Region C brigade were determined from the data we collected from schools and command organizations. For each brigade, instructor mandays are a function of both the "student-to-instructor" ratios for the courses taught and the ability of the system to achieve those ratios by efficiently matching instructors to courses.

To estimate the instructor days required for other than the FY95 student load, we assumed a constant linear relationship between instructor days and student load. In other words, we assumed that twice the student load would require twice the

---

[2]Mandays for training of instructors are considered under "variable staff days," discussed below.

instructor days, and half the student load would require half the instructor days. For example, since the CSS Brigade used 30 instructor days in FY95 for every 100 student days of training (as shown earlier in Figure 3.4), we assumed in the baseline model that the 30-per-100 ratio holds for all student loads. In subsequent runs of the model (discussed below), we assumed that a lower ratio could be achieved by employing strategies to increase efficiency.

TDA staff mandays. TDA staff refers to those personnel holding staff (noninstructor) positions on the school's TDA, plus authorized civilians. These functions can be described as administration (S1), operations (S3), logistics (S4), the command group, and the administrative staff for instructional battalions.

For the fiscal year training year, the number of TDA staff days was calculated based on the number of personnel assigned to TDA staff positions. To estimate TDA staff days for other student loads in the baseline model, we applied the rules used by the USAR for altering part-time and full-time staff,[3] then estimated a linear equation to smooth over stepwise relationships between staff and student load. The result is a relationship between TDA staff and student load that is far less than proportional. In other words, doubling student load requires far less than double the training manpower. For example, we estimate for the CSS Brigade that if the student load doubled, TDA staff days would increase by only 10 percent.

It is this relatively fixed element of school staffing that provides the opportunity for achieving easing Student Load to Planned L later in this section. Further, it is the estimated reduction of this staff that provides the opportunity for consolidating TDA staff positions also discussed later in this section.

Supplemental staff days. We include in "supplemental staff days" three elements: (1) borrowed staff days (i.e., all support needed above and beyond what TDA support personnel can provide); (2) days for individual training of all school personnel—including the battle-focused instructor training course (BFITC), small group instructor (SGI), and NCOES training of instructors; and (3) days required for special work projects (i.e., all ADSW used for nonteaching purposes, such as for conferences and evaluations).

---

[3]At the brigade level, part-time staff are considered fixed (although each brigade may be a little different) for all levels of student output. At the battalion level, extra part-time staff are authorized when the number of instructors supported exceeds 100. Generally, there is one new part-time position authorized for each 50 instructors over 100. The number of full-time staff (all civilian technicians in the USAR) at brigade level is generally one (except for the Health Services (HS) brigade, which has more full-time staff at the battalion level), but increases to two when the number of battalions supported is larger than four. Full-time staff at the battalion level is based on mission workload and unit size but does not often exceed two.

26

For the fiscal year training year, surveys showed that supplemental staff days were few in the USAR brigades for small student loads.

To estimate supplemental staff days for other student loads, we used ATRRS data and the results of our visits to AT sites during the assessment period.[4] First, supplemental staff required for additional students depends on whether those student days would come from weekend courses or AT courses. (Support requirements are typically much higher in the latter case.) We assumed that the ratio of weekend to AT training would stay the same as student load expanded or contracted.

Second, supplemental staff required for additional students depends on whether the additional training was accomplished by expanding the size of existing AT training sessions or by creating new training sessions (support requirements are typically much higher in the latter case). For example, for the CSS Brigade, we estimated that new ADT training sessions would require 12 supplemental staff days for every 100 student days, but that adding to existing ATs would require only 3 supplemental staff days for every 100 student days. For all AT training increases from the baseline, we assumed that half of any increase in student load would involve new ATs and half would expand the size of existing ATs.[5]

After adding all the components of manpower, we found that as student load increased, supplemental staff days increased substantially. For example, for doubling the CSS training load, we estimated that supplemental training days would have to triple.

Modeling Results

The final model is a linear approximation to the sum of the relationships for instructor mandays, TDA staff mandays, and supplemental staff days. In other words, adding the amounts of the three types of manpower discussed above for each brigade gives us a baseline total school mandays model. The total school mandays model estimates the staffing needs of an RC school at different levels of student load. For the CSS Brigade, the equation turns out to be

$$y = 4{,}117 + .40^*x \, ,$$

---

[4]We documented how much support manning was required for the entire AT and then obtained managers' estimates of how that number would differ for alternative-sized ATs.

[5]In addition, to account for additional schooling for training staff, we assumed that 20 percent of the days of any new staff would have to be used for their own training. To account for additional special work projects, we assumed that one staff day per hundred student days would have to be set aside for additional ADSW.

meaning that the brigade required 4,117 mandays of instructor and staff support, plus 40 days for every 100 student days. If one "plugs in" actual student days (21,800 for FY95) for x in the equation, then y equals actual school mandays, about 12,837, for the CS Brigade in FY95. Those 12,837 mandays are composed of 5,210 TDA staff mandays, 6,315 instructor mandays, and 1,312 supplemental mandays.

Dividing the total school mandays equation by 100x gives us a "school mandays per 100 student day" model, which we use to analyze school efficiency. In the case of the CSS Brigade, the equation is

$$y/100x = 40 + 41.17/x ,$$

meaning that school mandays per 100 student days will be 40 plus 41.17 divided by student load. As with the total school mandays equation, note that if one plugs in actual student days (21,800 for FY95) for x, then school mandays per 100 student days will approximate the actual efficiency—about 59 per 100 for FY95.

Figure 4.1 graphically represents the total school mandays curve and the school mandays per 100 student day curve for the CSS Brigade. These curves are somewhat comparable to the total cost and marginal cost curves described in basic economics textbooks.[6] The x-axis is student load, while the two y-axes represent school mandays per 100 student days (on the left) and total school mandays (on the right). The dashed lines show where the brigade actually operated on those curves in FY95: student load was 21,800 days, school mandays were 12,837, and the ratio of school mandays per 100 student days was 59.

While the total mandays curve shows an increase in school manpower with more students, the school mandays per 100 student day curve, which we use as a measure of efficiency, shows a decrease in the cost per student as student load increases (see Figure 4.1). The downward slope of this "efficiency" curve indicates the presence of economies of scale in school organizations.

Table 4.1 compares the model and FY95 information for the CSS, CS, and HS brigades. We see that the CS Brigade requires only about 6 percent more fixed and variable manpower than the CSS Brigade (i.e., variable mandays are only

---

[6]As general cost curves, both are somewhat oversimplified. For example, marginal cost curves are generally U-shaped, showing that resource constraints eventually negate the effects of scale economies. The more simplified shape of the curves we drew reflects the fact that we were unable to incorporate all the factors that increased cost as student load increased, for example the manpower cost of overcoming equipment and facilities shortages for large increases in student load. Preliminary sensitivity analysis showed that inserting reasonable factors would not change the general conclusions of this report. For purposes of the present report, such factors are accounted for in the discussion of results. Future versions of the models will take these factors into account more formally.

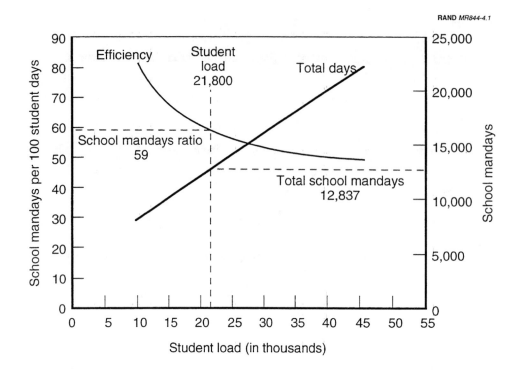

RAND *MR844-4.1*

Figure 4.1—The Total Days and Efficiency Curves, CSS Brigade, FY95

about 42.8 per 100, as opposed to 40 per 100); however, because the CS Brigade has a lower student load than the CSS Brigade (11,340 versus 21,800), the CS Brigade has a substantially less favorable efficiency (81 days versus 59). The HS Brigade requires considerably more variable manpower than either of the other two brigades (because of the lower student-to-instructor ratios required in medical-related courses) and has a relatively low student output. As a result, school mandays per 100 student days were considerably higher in the HS Brigade, over one and a half times the amount of the CSS Brigade.

Strategies for Achieving Improved Efficiency Through Capacity Use

We now turn to strategies for improving school efficiency. We consider each strategy individually (analyzing its effect on model parameters); we then look at the combined effect of employing all three strategies simultaneously. The results of the strategies are graphically illustrated using the CSS Brigade as the example; the tables provide data for both the CSS Brigade and the other brigades.

Table 4.1

FY95 Information for CSS, CS, and HS Brigades

Brigade	Model Parameters		Baseline Data		
	Fixed Staff Mandays (a)	Variable School Mandays/100 Student Days (b)	Student Days (x)	School Mandays (y)	School Mandays/ Student Days (y/x times 100)
CSS	4,117	40.0	21,800	12,837	59
CS	4,386	42.8	11,340	9,240	81
HS	1,773	66.1	3,686	4,209	116

Strategy 1: Consolidate TDA Staff

Efficiency can improve by reducing the number of personnel required in TDA staff positions (i.e., in administration, operations, logistics, etc.). A smaller TDA translates into fewer school mandays required for any given student load. In fact, during implementation of the prototype, the USAR designed a staff consolidation in the Region C school system when it reduced the number of administrative organizations from nine USARF schools to four school brigades. In the process of reducing the number of schools, TDAs shrank total part-time support staff by about a third.[7]

However, this planned consolidation in Region C was not fully implemented in FY95; while the number of schools was reduced to four brigades, the number of staff did not appreciably change. Had the results of the Region C consolidation been fully implemented, Figure 4.2 shows that given equivalent student load in the CSS Brigade (the vertical dashed line at 21,800), efficiency could have improved by about 12 percent—from the baseline 59 school mandays needed for each 100 student days of output (with schools operating partially under the old TDA) to 52 (under the new TDA). This is shown by the two horizontal dotted lines.

Figure 4.2 shows that the magnitude of the improvement to efficiency in the CSS Brigade depends on the starting point—the student load the brigade achieved in FY95 (21,800 student days). Beginning at smaller student loads would improve efficiency more, while beginning at higher student loads would improve efficiency less. The reason is that a fixed reduction in school staff is being spread over more units of output (i.e., student load).

---

[7]The TDA designed by the USAR is referred to as "Region C consolidation" in the following discussions.

30

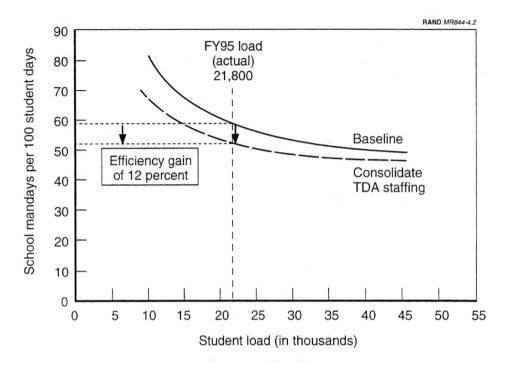

RAND *MR844-4.2*

Figure 4.2—Increase in Efficiency from Consolidation of RC Schools Staff
for the CSS Brigade

Table 4.2 shows that the potential of the USAR consolidation to improve efficiency is comparable across brigades. In the CS Brigade, the potential improvement is 10 percent, while in the HS Brigade it is 9 percent. Leadership and CA are not shown because no consolidation was planned; in fact, in the case of the latter, TDAs that fully cover requirements were being formulated at the time this report was prepared.

Achieving the potential efficiency gains of a reduction in TDA staff depends on designing more cost-effective work procedures to support training delivery. For example, staff workload and support costs could be reduced if fewer, more permanent training sites were established. An unrealistic "paper" consolidation would likely lead to, at best, a shift in the source of manpower—from less TDA manpower to more borrowed manpower—rather than to a real gain in efficiency. At worst, too much or the wrong kind of consolidation could lead to adverse effects on course quality and school responsiveness[8] and on student load.[9]

---

[8]In fact, our surveys showed that Region C's USAR brigades experienced problems in providing training support during FY95, especially for IDT. See the forthcoming RAND report on "Performance and Efficiency of the Total Army School System" for more discussion of these results.

[9]For example, if a reduction in support staff leads to problems in coordinating school locations and schedules with the units providing students, fewer students may attend courses.

31

Table 4.2

Increase in Efficiency of Planned USAR Consolidation for CSS, CS, and HS Brigades

Brigade	FY95 (Actual)			If Staff Is Reduced to TDA Levels			Efficiency Improvement
	Staff	Student Days	School Mandays/ 100 Student Days	Staff	Student Days	School Mandays/ 100 Student Days	
CSS	106	21,800	59	80	21,800	52	12%
CS	100	11,340	81	84	11,340	73	10%
HS	40	3,686	114	28	3,686	104	9%

SOURCE: RC schools survey, ATRRS, November 1995 TDAs.

More experience with the new system and additional transition resources to design improved work procedures will be required to achieve the estimated efficiencies from staff consolidation.

Strategy 2: Increase Student Throughput to Gain Scale Economies

Efficiency can also improve in RC schools by simply increasing student load to capture scale economies. As discussed above, scale economies exist because of the relatively fixed nature of TDA staff (i.e., doubling the student load does not double the TDA staff). As a result, as schools train more students, they are able to spread the fixed manpower needed to support training over more units of output.

Greater student load in schools can be achieved by improving the management of training requirements to ensure that more students who need training request it and attend classes. This ought to be possible, since our analysis has shown that there are large numbers of students who require training but do not receive it.[10] However, making this happen will require fully implementing the reservation system to the unit level.

How much student load can schools efficiently handle? Clearly, schools are currently operating at less than full capacity, since FY95 inputs are typically only about two-thirds of allocations, the amount schools agree they are able to train. Figure 4.3 shows the CSS Brigade baseline efficiency curve shown in Figures 4.1 and 4.2 at the actual student load (21,800, the first vertical dotted line) and at the

---

[10]See Winkler et al. (1996) for a discussion of the issue of scheduling students who require training.

32

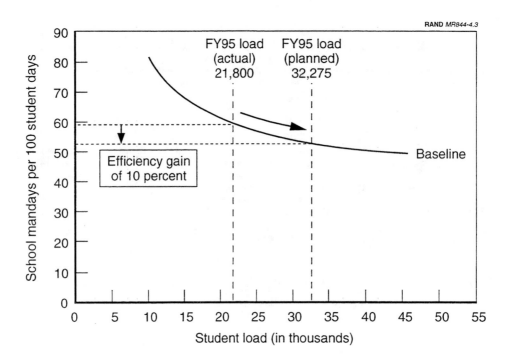

Figure 4.3—Increase in Efficiency from Increasing Student Load for the CSS Brigade

"planned student load" (32,275, the second vertical dotted line)—an amount nearly 50 percent higher than the actual load. The planned student load is assumed "achievable" because it represents the level of operation the schools agreed to when allocations were assigned. Increasing student load in the CSS Brigade to the planned student load level (32,275) yields a 10 percent efficiency gain (from 59 to 53).[11]

Other training organizations in Region C could realize even greater economy-of-scale gains than the CSS Brigade, largely because they are smaller organizations to begin with. Smaller organizations begin at smaller student loads, where their efficiency curve is steepest and where gains in student load have the largest effect on efficiency. Table 4.3 shows the estimated effects on efficiency for two of the other USAR brigades. The CS Brigade, with only about half the FY95 student load as the CSS Brigade, could realize an efficiency gain of 17 percent, almost double the CSS gain. Similarly, the HS Brigade, with about 17 percent of the CSS student load, could improve by 19 percent.

---

[11]To isolate the effect of scale economies, the 10 percent efficiency gain shows only the improvement possible from increasing student load. It does not consider potential improvements in instructor utilization (an issue considered in the next subsection). In particular, the calculation assumes that the 50 percent increase in student load will require an equivalent 50 percent increase in instructor days.

Table 4.3

Increase in Efficiency from Increasing Student Load to Planned Level
for CSS, CS, and HS Brigades

Brigade	FY95 (Actual)			If Student Load Is Increased to Planned Level			Efficiency Improvement
	Student Days	School Mandays	School Mandays/ 100 Student Days	Student Days	School Mandays	School Mandays/ 100 Student Days	
CSS	21,800	12,837	59	32,275	17,027	53	10%
CS	11,340	9,240	81	18,226	12,187	67	17%
HS	3,686	4,209	114	6,941	6,361	92	19%

SOURCE: RC schools survey, ATRRS.

ARNG school organizations. Despite a large total output (about 20,000), the ARNG's CA Brigade could still likely benefit greatly from scale economies by expanding its student load. The brigade is now composed of four smaller administrative organizations (the former SMAs of the region). Each of the smaller organizations has its own relatively fixed TDA staff and averages about 5,000 student days in output, nearly 23 percent of the total CSS student load. The small size of the organizations suggests that each is operating on a relatively steep part of its efficiency curve, where expansion could bring the greatest gains in efficiency.

The RTS-Ms, technically part of the CSS Brigade but run by the ARNG, could also realize scale economies. Despite their large size, most indicated they operated at well below their full physical capacity (and a comparison of allocations to inputs supports those statements) and that reaching full capacity would require little or no increase in support manpower.

In contrast to the other Region C organizations, the ARNG's Leadership Brigade cannot likely gain efficiency from scale economies. Although data on quotas suggest that the brigade currently operates at less than full capacity, NCO training has been decreasing and is likely to decrease more in the future as "select-train-promote" policies are fully implemented.

Absent the closing of institutions, realizing scale economies in the school system depends on the proposition that more qualified students can consistently be brought to the schools. While requirements data (e.g., showing large numbers of non-duty-MOS-qualified soldiers) suggest that schools could train more students and Region C TDAs imply an increase in the number of instructors, realizing higher inputs will require an improved system for identifying requirements and ensuring that soldiers needing training reach school.[12] In fact, if schools hire to their TDAs but cannot bring in more students, efficiency will decrease rather than increase.

Strategy 3: Improve the Match of Instructors to Inputs to Yield Optimal Mix

Efficiency can improve by changing the composition of instructor manpower to better match training inputs. For maximum efficiency, schools would like to have exactly the right number of instructors available for each training session, given the number of inputs for each class. With too few instructors, schools have to cancel courses and thereby lose scale economies. With too many instructors, either instructors get reassigned to nonteaching tasks or student/instructor ratios fall below optimal levels. In either case, fewer students receive training than instructors could potentially handle.

Achieving maximum efficiency with instructors requires policies and procedures that lead to (1) TDAs with instructor positions that reflect long-term training demand by skill area and training level; (2) sufficient supplemental resources to staff short-term surges or spikes in demand; (3) timely and accurate forecasts (i.e., quotas) of inputs; (4) high fill rates once quotas are established; and (5) school management practices that involve hiring the right number of instructors and successfully matching them to specific courses and the right number of students.

How well were instructors matched to students in FY95, and what improvements might be expected in the future? Below we approximate what the training system achieved in FY95; we then construct an example to show how efficiency could potentially improve.

An examination of the FY95 training year in Region C found ample evidence of lost potential because of instructor surpluses. These surpluses occurred when classes failed to achieve the minimum size needed to conduct training and when fewer students showed up for courses than what was indicated by quotas. Table 4.4 compares, for both weekend and AT training, the number of organic and borrowed instructors the schools actually had with the number required given actual inputs. To determine required instructors for the FY95 student load, we applied course-specific instructor-student ratios[13] to the inputs of individual

---

[12]Realizing an expansion will also require surmounting the challenges of equipment and facility limitations.

[13]The predominant optimum ratio for classes is one instructor per 10 students. However, the ratio can become much lower for some technical courses (e.g., 1:6 for a medical specialist, MOS 91B) or much higher for other courses suitable to larger-group instruction (e.g., 1:20 for a Personnel Administration Specialist, MOS 75B).

Table 4.4

Instructor Surpluses Given Inputs, Region C, FY95

| Battalion/ Brigade | Number of Instructors | | | | | |
| | Weekend Training | | | AT Training | | |
	Actual[a]	Required[b]	Ratio	Actual	Required	Ratio
Leadership	207	77	2.7	750[c]	398	1.9
Personnel Service	47	30	1.6	47	16	2.9
Chemical	31	12	2.6	31	13	2.4
Health Services	34	13	2.6	34	28	1.2
Quartermaster	53	32	1.7	58	33	1.8
Engineer	12	10	1.2	12	6	2.0
Transportation	30	26	1.2	42	42	1.0
Military Police	12	14	.9	12	12	1.0
Signal	29	33	.9	29	31	.9

[a]Includes borrowed and excludes lent instructors.

[b]Assumes inputs are known in advance and optimal student-instructor ratios.

[c]Number here refers to instructor periods, assuming a full-time instructor teaches 12 periods.

SOURCE: The DOLFINS data system (supplemented with appendixes to Group AT orders) supplied information on the actual number of instructors used.

classes.[14] While some battalions, like military police and signal, ended up with the right number of instructors (sometimes after borrowing), most battalions had more instructors than required, often more than twice the requirement. In addition, some battalions had an imbalanced weekend and AT training load. For example, the engineer battalion needed only 6 instructors for AT but required 10 for IDT.[15]

The Leadership Brigade had the largest surplus of instructors, more than twice the required number given inputs. This was the result of a steep decline of inputs that was not fully captured when instructors were assigned to schools. Student load decreased tremendously for a number of reasons, including (1) a more selective policy on which soldiers could take NCOES courses, (i.e., the implementation of the "select-train-promote" policy); (2) enforcement of a new, more demanding physical fitness standard (i.e., the AFPT test) that sent many

---

[14]For example, given an optimum student-instructor ratio of 1:16 in the BNCOC Phase I course, one instructor would be required for any class size up to 16, two would be required for any class size between 17 and 32, etc.

[15]The problem of managing instructors is even more complex than the table implies. While instructors are listed at the battalion or brigade level of detail, managers must also match skill requirements within battalions. For example, the transportation battalion may have the right number of total instructors, but it also needs an appropriate number qualified to teach at least five different specialties—motor transport operator, traffic management coordinator, cargo specialist, watercraft operator, and watercraft engineer—at three different training levels. Further, for IDT, schools must not only obtain the right type of instructors, they must also find them in locations near the students needing that type of instruction.

registered students home from the course before it started; and (3) a ruling during the school's accreditation that reduced the number of locations where the weekend versions of ANCOC and BNCOC could be offered.

A better matching of instructors to inputs would have led to substantial efficiency improvements. To define an "optimal" match of instructors, we assumed that for any given student load in a skill area, schools would need the required number of instructors (given class size and student/instructor ratios as defined by the program of instruction (POI)) plus 20 percent. In other words, we assumed that for every 10 instructors required in a skill area, the school would hire 12 instructors to maintain sufficient flexibility to cover the workload.

Figure 4.4 shows the estimated improvement in efficiency for the CSS Brigade if instructors are optimally matched to students (as defined above). In the lower curve shown in the figure, fewer instructor days are required for any given student load because instructors are teaching more students on average, thus increasing student-instructor ratios. Conversely, the lower curve implies that any given set of instructors would produce a greater student load.

To illustrate potential efficiency improvements from better instructor matching, we chose the scenario of keeping the FY95 instructor pool and skill mix and

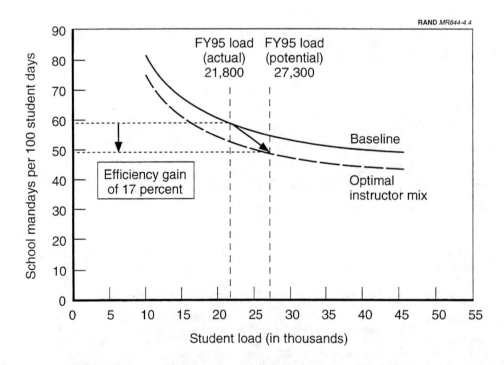

Figure 4.4—Increase in Efficiency from Improved Instructor Utilization for the CSS Brigade

assuming that enough students had attended classes so that those instructors would be optimally utilized. The rightmost vertical dotted line in Figure 4.4 shows the resulting increase in student load for the CSS Brigade—to 27,300 days. The arrow in the chart shows the improvement in efficiency (and increase in student load) possible if all FY95 instructors in the CSS brigade had been optimally utilized. The improvement was from the base number of 59 to 49, an improvement of 17 percent.

Table 4.5 shows the comparable results for the CS, HS, and Leadership brigades, as well as the change in school mandays that occurred in the process. Although the number of instructors was held constant at the FY95 level for the present illustration, school mandays do increase somewhat because of the supplemental staff needed to support the additional students instructors could handle.

In other brigades, the potential for improving efficiency through optimal utilization of their FY95 instructor pools varies widely. In the CS Brigade, there is essentially no potential improvement; there, the problem was finding enough instructors rather than fully utilizing the ones they had. In the HS Brigade, efficiency would improve an estimated 17 percent, an amount comparable to the CSS Brigade.

Potential improvement in the Leadership Brigade (shown in the last row of Table 4.5) exceeded 27 percent, but in this case we assumed that achieving the improvement does not lie in enrolling more students. In contrast to courses taught in the other brigades, leadership courses do not have a large associated untrained requirement. Instead, we assumed that the key to improving instructor utilization in the leadership area lies in reducing the number of instructors. As discussed above, the number of instructors assigned to the

Table 4.5

Increase in Efficiency from Improved Instructor Utilization for CSS, CS, HS, and Leadership Brigades

Brigade	FY95 (Actual)			If Instructor Mix Is Optimal			Efficiency Improvement
	Student Days	School Mandays	School Mandays/100 Student Days	Student Days	School Mandays	School Mandays/100 Student Days	
CSS	21,800	12,837	59	27,300	13,481	49	17%
CS	11,340	9,240	81	11,500	9,308	81	0%
HS	3,686	4,209	114	4,720	4,468	95	17%
Leadership	56,780	29,442	52	56,780	21,515	38	27%

SOURCE: RC schools survey, ATRRS, DOLFINS (supplemented with appendixes to Group AT orders).

38

leadership mission far exceeded inputs. For example, according to the ANCOC
and BNCOC programs of instruction (POIs), each instructor could handle 16
students in a class; but in FY95, there was an instructor potentially available for
about every 5 students in weekend classes, and one for every 8 students in AT
classes. In fact, for the AT phases of training at Leesburg, none of the 200+
instructors supplied by the USAR would have been required to complete the
mission. Thus, Table 4.5 shows an improvement in efficiency based on an
unchanging student load but a reduction in instructors sufficient to realize an
optimal match of instructors to students.

The number of instructors assigned to the leadership mission in FY95 was
determined by TDA authorizations in that area. As other brigades begin to fill
instructor positions determined by the new TDAs, the correctness of those
authorizations becomes critical to school efficiency. TDA authorizations should
be based on the expected number of requirements by skill area and on estimates
of the number of those requirements who will enroll in classes any given year.
Table 4.6 compares the skill level of instructors in the current TDAs with FY95
training requirements. Note that there are large variations in the ratio.

In the absence of more precise data on requirements, current TDAs have been
based on historical enrollments (notably unreliable), on predictions of future
enrollments, and on expert opinion of future demand. The current uncertainties
in estimating the demand for training by skill area argue for infusing extra
flexibility in RC TDAs. When schools end up with fewer or more instructor
positions than they originally thought they would need, maintaining efficiency
requires supporting the ability of the schools to make near-term adjustments in a
timely manner. For example, if surplus instructors are discovered in the

Table 4.6

Training and Instructor Requirements Versus TDA Authorizations, Region C, FY95

Battalion	Training Requirements	Instructors Needed	TDA Instructor Authorizations	Ratio Authorized/ Needed
Chemical	274	33	30	.91
Engineer	625	95	41	.43
Military Police	255	25	61	2.44
Signal	680	99	92	.93
Medical	864	122	99	.81
Personnel Service	880	79	78	.99
Quartermaster	1,327	138	113	.82
Transportation	939	88	101	1.15

SOURCE: SIDPERS, USAR December 1995 TDAs.

leadership area in the future, training brigades need an ability to quickly reassign extra instructors (based on their MOS) to brigades that have a greater need.

Other strategies can be employed that lead to better student-instructor matches. For example, one way to accomplish higher fill rates is to make the reservation system more flexible by, for example, allowing controlled overbooking. In addition, for planning purposes and for hiring the right instructors, schools could be supplied with more information than they are currently receiving. One critical piece of information is student location for IDT requirements (when available) to help schools hire the right instructors. Schools used to get this information through the now-defunct STRIPES process; now that information might come from ATRRS. Another critical piece is additional information about instructors outside their own organization. Responsiveness and flexibility can be enhanced if schools are better able to identify and obtain qualified instructors as they are needed (e.g., through a centralized instructor registry).

Combined Effect of Strategies

Figure 4.5 looks at the effects on the CSS Brigade of implementing the three strategies simultaneously. As in earlier figures, the top curve in the chart represents the baseline that approximates the operating realities of FY95 and the dashed vertical line to the left marks the actual FY95 student load and the efficiency achieved (21,800; 59). The lower curve and dashed vertical line to the right represent the effects of combining strategies. It assumes the implementation of the planned consolidation of TDA staff, the successful conversion of all planned quotas into students attending courses, and the near optimization of instructor utilization. At the point where the right vertical line intersects the curve (at 32,275), the instructor utilization is higher because class "fill rates" increase to the level specified by the allocations and because instructors were often already available to teach classes no longer assumed canceled or nonconducted. Under these conditions, efficiency would have improved from 59 to 45, a 24 percent improvement.

To cite an upper-bound estimate, an even greater improvement in efficiency would be possible if all the instructors in the FY96 TDA have been hired and fully utilized. In FY95, less than half the instructors authorized in the new TDA were assigned to schools. Assuming a future state where all those authorizations have been filled and assuming that they could all be optimally utilized,[16] the

---

[16]Achieving that great a student load would clearly involve not only challenges of matching instructors to students, but also challenges in obtaining required equipment and facilities.

40

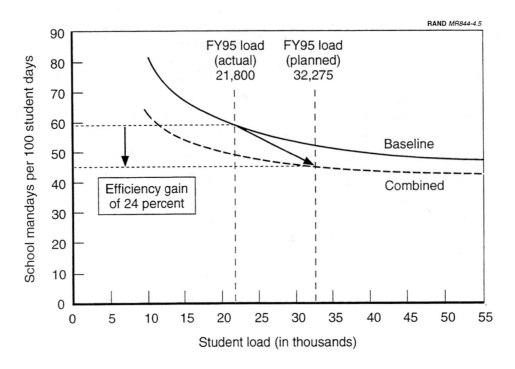

RAND *MR844-4.5*

Figure 4.5—Increase in Efficiency from Combining Strategies for the CSS Brigade

CSS Brigade would achieve a student load of over 57,000 (162 percent higher than the FY95 student load) and an efficiency gain of 34 percent—from 59 to 39 school mandays per 100 student days.

Table 4.7 compares the effects of combining strategies in the CS Brigade and HS Brigade with the results in the CSS Brigade. The CS Brigade could attain about the same improvement (25 percent), but the key there is increased student load rather than improved instructor utilization. The HS brigade could realize efficiency gains from both increasing student load and improving instructor utilization. Combining both strategies could realize a higher total gain—about 32 percent.

The magnitude of the efficiency results from combining strategies is not unique to these brigades; other brigades can match or surpass these results as well. For example, we have seen that the Leadership Brigade could have improved efficiency almost as much as the CSS Brigade, just by reducing the number of surplus instructors assigned to the mission. The CA Brigade can increase efficiency by increasing student throughput in the various organizations that make up the brigade.

Table 4.7

Increase in Efficiency by Combining Strategies for CSS, CS, and HS Brigades

Brigade	FY95 (Actual)			If All Strategies Are Combined			Efficiency Improve-ment
	Student Days	School Mandays	School Mandays/ Student Day	Planned Student Days	School Mandays	School Mandays/ Student Day	
CSS	21,800	12,837	.59	32,275	14,615	.45	24%
CS	11,340	9,240	.81	18,226	11,164	.61	25%
HS	3,686	4,209	1.14	6,941	5,356	.77	32%

SOURCE: RC schools survey, ATRRS, DOLFINS (supplemented with appendixes to Group AT orders).

Conclusions

We believe that substantial increases in efficiency are possible from undertaking three strategies: (1) consolidating TDA staff (e.g., along the lines of the planned USAR consolidation); (2) increasing student load by bringing more of the students needing training to the schoolhouse; and (3) improving the course-by-course matching of instructors to students. Concerning the latter strategy, it is important to note that the keys to future efficiency are making reliable predictions of course enrollment, filling those classes once scheduled, and infusing flexibility in school TDAs to make the specification of instructor positions responsive to changes in training requirements and student enrollments.

It is also important to note that the above improvements in efficiency depend on how the training is implemented and managed on the ground. For example, the success of the USAR consolidation of staff manpower depends on developing work procedures that effectively support training without sacrificing course quality or school responsiveness. Moreover, if the larger training system is successful in bringing more training requirements to the schoolhouse, the increased training load will challenge the ground-level management and coordinating system to efficiently obtain sufficient instructors, equipment, facilities, and training areas to implement that training.

To ensure that future changes at all levels of the training system realize efficiency improvements will require an information system to monitor year-to-year outcomes. The beginnings of such a system are addressed in the appendix to this report.

5. Increasing Efficiency by Consolidating Training Sites

The old school system was criticized for redundancy—for offering courses at too many locations, which duplicates effort and wastes support resources. The movement toward the new school system in Region C was partially motivated by these concerns, and, indeed, specialization induced by the new Region C school system has already reduced the number of AT training locations by 41 percent (see Figure 3.1). Moreover, the ARNG has considered the creation of "superregional" sites for training in specific career fields.

However, despite the promise of consolidation, there is concern about the effect that training site consolidation will have on training resources and efficiency, particularly travel. Fewer training sites will mean longer travel distances for students and instructors and, therefore, higher travel costs, which could offset or even exceed any gains in support.

Thus, the question is, how many locations for particular types of courses are ideal? Should there be one AT covering every kind of course in every region, more than one AT per region, or less than one (i.e., superregional sites)? For IDT training the questions are similar, but the focus changes from a national one to a local one. Can the number of IDT weekend training sites be productively reduced while still keeping the distance students have to travel from their homes reasonable?

In this section we explore whether the consolidation of AT sites or IDT training sites can bring about *net* gains in efficiency. We start with a discussion of how we extended our methodology to address this issue, and then examine the net effects of fewer training sites, first in the context of AT training, then in the context of IDT weekend training.

Methodology

Consolidating a dispersed system of training locations involves a tradeoff: While support manpower can decrease by consolidating training to a smaller number of locations, fewer training sites will mean longer travel distances for students and instructors and, therefore, higher travel costs. If the increase in travel costs is less than the decrease in support costs, then total costs decrease and the consolidation in sites yields efficiency.[1] This tradeoff relationship is captured by what is, in most situations, a U-shaped total cost curve, where total cost is defined as the sum of travel costs and support costs per student. The total cost curve, which becomes our new measure of efficiency, shows that higher costs (and lower efficiency) occur with either too many or too few sites, and that minimum cost (and maximum efficiency) is obtained by using a middle number of training locations—one that balances travel and support cost.

Modeling the tradeoff between manpower support costs and travel costs requires adding four new pieces to the methodology discussed in Section 4. First, we convert training support days into dollars so they can be compared to travel costs. Using existing TDAs as a guide and factors obtained from CEAC that estimate pay and benefits (including retirement), we assume that the average instructor was pay grade E-7 and the average staff person was pay grade E-6.

Second, to estimate training support manpower costs as a function of the number of locations, we once again draw on the results of our visits to AT sites during the assessment period. During those visits, we documented the support manpower actually used for the AT in question, then obtained managers' estimates on how that number would change for alternative-sized ATs and sequentially run ATs. Larger ATs were typically predicted to realize large savings in support; for example, increasing the size of the AT by 50 percent would often require only about a 5 percent increase in support manpower. Sequential ATs, for which setup and closedown costs could be avoided, yielded significant but much more modest efficiencies. When modeling the reduction of support costs per 100 student days as a function of the reduction in the number of sites, we assume gaining sites will expand by using a combination of larger training sessions and a greater number of sequential training sessions.

Third, to estimate the distance traveled by students and instructors as a function of the number of locations, we begin with the current number of locations at which a course or set of courses was taught and the average distances traveled by instructors and students. To estimate the distance students would travel if the number of sites were higher or lower, we employed a mathematical formula that relates the number of sites and distance. The formula states that after a change, the new average distance would equal the old distance times the ratio of the

---

[1]This argument assumes that the demand for training is unaffected by the consolidation of training locations. If an increase in travel costs or a reduction in course frequency leads to fewer enrollments and more untrained requirements, the consolidation would have an efficiency cost in terms of reduced RC readiness. A commitment by decisionmakers to fully fund any increases in travel cost associated with the consolidation should eliminate any potential effect of travel cost on the demand for training. The possible effect of reduced course frequency on the demand for training is an issue that would require additional research.

44

original number of sites to the new number of sites. Thus, if the original number of locations was eight, the average distance traveled would double at four locations (half the original number), and double again at two locations (half again the number of locations).[2]

Finally, to calculate the cost of travel, we assumed 30 cents per mile as the amount the military would have to pay for additional travel generated by a reduction in the number of training sites. To obtain a basis for this estimate, we turn to the USAR's DOLFINS data base, collecting actual personnel payments in FY94 for trips originating from Region C, Region E, and (to provide some national perspective) two western regions—Utah and California. The summary of these estimates (see Table 5.1) shows that the military paid somewhat less than 30 cents per mile in three of four regions for nonair travel and in two of four regions for air travel.[3] However, because figures do not include out-of-pocket costs, total travel costs will be higher than what the military paid. We decided to use 30 cents per mile as an approximate standard for our analyses, higher than that implied by Table 5.1, because we assumed that any changes in the school system that lead to increased travel costs would have to be fully reimbursed by the military.

While there is no actual data for IDT travel, we assumed that students and instructors would be reimbursed at the going rate of 30 cents per mile for any portion of a trip that exceeded 50 miles. For the issues addressed here, our general conclusions were insensitive to these simplifying assumptions.

Consolidating AT Sites Can Provide Net Efficiency Gains

In conducting our analysis, we found that having less than one AT training location per region for a course (the so-called superregional training sites) is efficient when support costs are high. This analysis tends to support the ARNG

---

[2]In using this formula, we first had to adjust for crossovers—personnel who "crossed over" the class closest to them to attend a class at a more distant site (presumably for the schedule convenience). We assumed that as the number of sites decreased the proportion of crossover would decrease. This adjustment flattened the travel cost curve but turned out to be insensitive to the conclusions of our analyses.

[3]Even though Table 5.1 shows that the military paid more travel expenses when air travel was involved, the figures do not imply that air travel is more expensive. First, in a substantial number of "nonair travel" cases, the military personnel account paid nothing at all or much less than the true cost, either because the student bore some of the costs himself or travel was provided by military vehicle. Second, for the more distant training that involves air travel, commands may more often have to pay per diem during the training period, because it is more difficult to arrange government housing and food.

Table 5.1

Student Travel Costs per Mile

Region	Average Trip Cost[a] ($)	Average Travel and Per Diem ($)	Percent Travel and Per Diem[b]	Average One-Way Distance (miles)	Average Cost/Mile (cents)[b]
Nonair travel					
Region C	1,000	158	16	305	26
Region E	1,162	247	21	413	30
Utah	1,043	158	15	339	23
California	1,089	216	20	513	21
Air travel					
Region C	1,617	692	43	1,021	34
Region E	1,388	573	41	801	36
Utah	1,507	601	40	1,072	28
California	1,324	436	33	1,002	22

SOURCE: USAR DOLFINS data system, FY94.

[a]Includes pay, allowances, and travel costs. Travel periods of 8–19 days are included.

[b]Numbers are rounded.

plan of superregional sites for CA courses. Such a plan may also make sense for other types of courses.

Figure 5.1 illustrates our results for one such CA course, the 11M AT. The y-axis represents the cost per student per AT and the x-axis the number of training sites. The middle curve shows the decreasing cost of support on a per-student basis as the number of training sites decreases, allowing more focused support and more students per AT. While that cost is nearly $900 per student with eight training sites (corresponding to one site per region), it decreases to less than $600 per student if all training can be consolidated to two sites. In contrast, the lowest curve shows the increasing cost of travel as the number of sites decreases. While that cost averages only $200 with eight locations (average one-way distance 300 miles), it increases to $500 per student with two locations (average one-way distance 750 miles). The highest curve is the total U-shaped cost curve, which at each point shows the sum of travel and support cost. The curve shows higher costs occurring with either too large or too small a number of sites. The lowest point along the curve is at about four sites, which implies about one site for every two TASS regions.

Just how much can be saved by consolidating training sites depends on the starting point. If the current number of sites is far from the optimal number, high savings are possible; but if the current number is equal to the optimum, no savings are possible. In the case of the 11M AT example, modest savings derive from consolidation. As shown in the figure, the number of 11M AT sites in FY95

RAND *MR844-5.1*

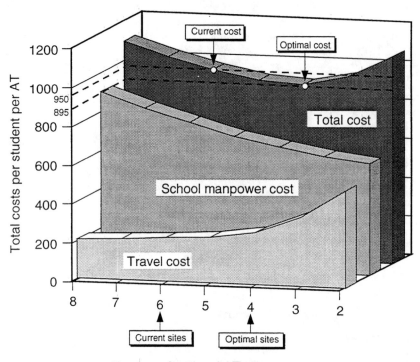

Based on prototype assessment data on 11M AT

Figure 5.1—Consolidating AT Sites Can Provide Further Efficiency Gains

was six, but it would appear possible to reduce the number of AT locations from six to about four (in the lowest point of the U-shaped curve) to achieve about 7 percent savings (reducing total cost from $950 to $895 per student).[4] Reducing beyond four sites causes travel costs to escalate much faster than it causes support costs to fall and, thus, leads to another less than optimal situation.

We suspect there may be other such courses where the number of AT training locations could be reduced to improve efficiency and reduce the total cost of training. For example, we found the 13B40 course to require more than twice the support that the 11M AT required. However, outside CA and perhaps medical support, the number of courses for which superregional sites makes economic sense may be small. For example, for personnel service courses such as 71L, support costs are too low initially for superregional sites to save enough to offset

---

[4]Drawing this conclusion with certainty would require data on the actual travel distances of potential students and on the training support costs at the sites involved. This illustrative example was constructed based on the two 11M ATs that RAND attended in Region C and E in FY94, and may not accurately portray the national picture.

increased travel costs. In fact, in those cases, multiple training sites per region may well be the least-cost option.

Finally, it is worth noting that the matching of students to training locations might be improved without having to trade off support costs and travel costs. When we examine training locations, if the current distribution of training sites is suboptimal, the number of sites might be redistributed without an increase in travel cost. For example, we showed that the number of training locations in Region C was reduced by 41 percent (in Figure 3.1), but that reduction was implemented without increasing the average distance students traveled (see Table 2.1). When we examine student behavior, our FY94 data show that students often travel longer distances than required to attend the course that they need. For example, we found that in FY95, more than a quarter of the Region E students attending AT traveled long distances outside their region, even though the course they took was offered within their region at a different time during the year.

Travel Costs Limit the Benefits of Consolidating Weekend Training Sites

Weekend mode (IDT) training has generally followed the philosophy of dispersion rather than consolidation—that is, bringing the training to the student, rather than sending the students to the training. From an efficiency point of view, it makes sense to send one instructor to ten students rather than make ten students travel to the instructor. In addition, when the IDT site is the student's location, that unit can typically easily supply "free" support for the training.

However, others argue that such dispersed training goes too far, that courses become duplicative and lead to smaller-than-minimum class sizes. For example, consolidating two proximate training sites might be more efficient if one instructor can teach a class of 10 students rather than having two instructors teaching classes of 5 each. Added to the instructor savings would be savings in support—one IDT site would require half the staff manpower to support that two would. While fewer IDT sites in an area will likely mean somewhat longer travel times for some instructors and students, manpower savings, the argument goes, would be enough to cover any increases in travel cost.

We found that the data did not support the argument for the consolidation of IDT training sites. First, we found that for higher-density MOS (where consolidation would be a potential option), small class sizes were relatively rare. Instead, most small classes occurred within low-density MOS, where only one or a handful of classes were being taught within a region. As a result, we conclude that significant instructor cost savings from consolidation are unlikely.

48

Second, for most IDT courses, potential support cost savings would be too small to justify the increases in travel cost that consolidation would bring. Savings in support manpower are small because so little is required in the first place— sometimes only an hour or two of a few people's time.[5] Figure 5.2 shows two possible total cost curves (comparable to the total cost curves of Figure 5.1). The lower curve represents the situation most IDT courses face and assumes eight hours of support for a course spread over a weekend. The requirement for this amount of support was reported by an SMA in Region E; for other schools (e.g., the Personnel Services Battalion of the CSS Brigade), even less support was reported. Even with this relatively "high" level of support, the lower curve in Figure 5.2 shows that minimum cost is not reached at fewer than 16 sites per region. Costs increase significantly from there as the number of sites is reduced. Once again, the reason is that the increase in travel costs[6] from consolidation overwhelms the support savings. As a result, we conclude the traditional practice of "bringing the training to the student" still makes economic sense.

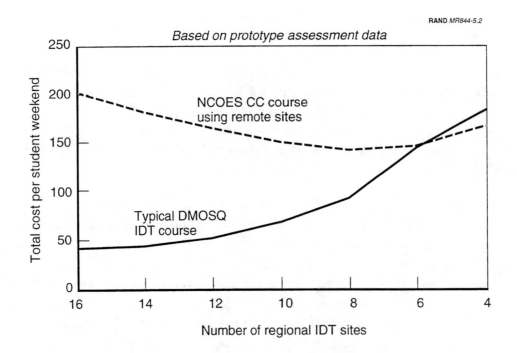

Figure 5.2—But Travel Costs Limit the Benefits of Consolidating
Weekend Training Sites

---

[5]This does not mean that the support problem in IDT courses can be ignored—a mechanism for borrowing equipment (comparable to the existing 156R process used for AT courses) still needs to be put in place. However, it does mean that consolidating locations will not make the task significantly easier.

[6]While the chart shows that the reduction in training sites leads to an increase in travel costs, in practice the effect of potentially higher travel costs is more likely lower student attendance.

Generally, the more dispersed the better, at least to the point where minimum required class sizes can be achieved.[7]

The upper curve in Figure 5.2 shows a rare but important exception to the typical IDT scenario, one where fewer sites are justified. The U-shaped curve represents the cost of operating NCOES common core courses (e.g., BNCOC) on remote bases in Region C. The curve was constructed by assuming it would take 8–10 full-time people per location to open sites currently shut down on weekends. Each site would support 50–100 students. Support costs of that magnitude were, in fact, potentially faced by the Leadership Brigade in Region C after its proponent school (USASMA) began a policy requiring BNCOC to be taught in a military environment, complete with barracks and other facilities to support an overnight stay. Unless enough sites could be found that were currently operational on the weekend to accommodate course demands, the USASMA requirements would significantly increase the support burden for the course. In fact, the Leadership Brigade found only five such sites suitable for the FY96 training year; as Figure 5.2 shows, the optimum number appears to be around eight.[8]

Conclusions

Based on the data we collected and the relationships we observed, we believe that efficiency could improve by consolidating some high-support courses—particularly high-support AT courses. To achieve these efficiencies in support manning, decisionmakers must be willing to pay somewhat more for travel costs; however, some increases in travel costs can be mitigated by reducing traveling out of region to take training. Further, while we have shown that too much consolidation can be as inefficient as not enough consolidation, we have provided a framework for conducting analyses to determine the most efficient number of locations on a course-by-course basis.

---

[7]These findings do not consider the potential gains in efficiency from "distance learning" technology, since such technology is not likely to be available on a large scale in the near future.

[8]Before the change in policy, BNCOC resembled a typical IDT course in terms of support needs and was conducted at a large number of sites (53 sites in Region C in FY94 and 28 in FY95). However, while this analysis provides a framework for analyzing the BNCOC location issue, determining exactly what to do about BNCOC (and ANCOC) weekend locations for future years will require more analysis given the fast-changing nature of NCOES training.

6. Recommendations

The results of our assessment indicate that efficiency can improve in the RC
school system. Given the fact that the school system is currently falling far short
of meeting the current RC training demand, we describe efficiency gains not in
terms of fewer dollars or other resource savings, but primarily in terms of an
increased utilization of the system's key resource—manpower. However, even if
experience should show that more of the soldiers requiring training cannot be
brought to the schoolhouse, we believe significant efficiency improvement can be
realized in terms of reductions of school manpower and other resources.[1] All but
one of our recommendations for improving efficiency in the school system still
apply if student load does not increase.

To summarize our recommendations, efficiency in the school system can
improve if more soldiers can be brought to the RC schools and if the match
between instructors and students can improve to achieve larger class sizes and
more optimally utilized instructors. The match between instructors and students
will get better if predictions of student inputs can be made more accurate, if
better information can be provided to schools for hiring instructors, and if the
school manpower system (principally the school TDA structure) can be made
more flexible for responding to unpredicted changes in demand. To a lesser
extent, we also see improvements in efficiency from regionalizing ATs for high-
support courses. Finally, to ensure future improvements in efficiency, we see the
need for sufficient supplemental resources to design more cost-effective work
procedures to support the consolidation of training staffs, and we recommend
the development of a tracking system to monitor efficiency. Below we discuss
each of these recommendations in more detail.

Train More Soldiers to Capture Scale Economies

Our analysis has concluded that because of the scale economies present in RC
schools, they can make large gains in efficiency just by increasing their student
load to take advantage of their underutilized capacity. Moreover, an increase in
student throughput ought to be possible, since our analysis has shown that there

---

[1]For ARNG schools, manpower may have to be added to the school system even if the total
manpower used per student can go down. The reason is that prior to the TASS reorganization,
ARNG schools operated primarily on borrowed military manpower.

are large numbers of students who require training but do not attend.[2] Therefore, achieving efficiencies in the school system requires improving the management of training requirements to ensure that more students who need training request it. Making this happen requires fully implementing the reservation system to the unit level.

Improve the Match Between Instructors and Students

Our analysis also revealed that a second strategy for increasing the efficiency of the school system is to improve the match between the instructors available and the students who show up for training. Current mismatches can largely be traced to erroneous predictions of student input. Research has suggested that the less allocations change, the greater the ability of the schools to have the right instructors when the classes begin. Therefore, for the school system to plan and schedule training more efficiently, more accurate and timely estimates of student inputs are needed.

Given the limits of improving predictions in the RC system,[3] schools can employ other strategies that lead to better student-instructor matches. For example, one way to accomplish higher fill rates is to make the reservation system more flexible by, for example, allowing controlled overbooking. In addition, for planning purposes and for hiring the right instructors, schools could be supplied with more information than they are currently receiving. One critical piece is student location for IDT requirements (when available) to help schools hire the right instructors. Schools used to get this information through the now-defunct STRIPES process; now that information might come from ATRRS. Another critical piece is additional information about instructors outside their own organization. Responsiveness and flexibility can be enhanced if schools are better able to identify and obtain qualified instructors as they are needed (e.g., through a centralized instructor registry).

Finally, the match between instructors and students can be further improved by refining and infusing additional flexibility into TDAs and by ensuring that schools have sufficient supplemental resources to efficiently respond to short-term change. Both of these ideas are discussed under separate headings below.

---

[2]See Winkler et al. (1996) for a discussion of the issue of scheduling students who require training.

[3]For example, to plan for IDT training, accurate predictions of student load are required down to the local level of detail.

Regionalize (and Sometimes Nationalize) AT for High-Support Courses, But Not IDT

Our analysis has suggested that consolidating training sites for high-support courses will yield net efficiencies to the training system in the AT arena, but not in the IDT one.[4] To achieve these efficiencies in support manning, decisionmakers must be willing to pay somewhat more for travel costs; however, some increases in travel costs can be mitigated by reducing traveling out of region to take training.

These conclusions support the ARNG initiative of creating superregional sites for the AT phases of high-support CA courses and suggest that other courses might benefit from similar moves.[5] However, we also conclude that a balance is required—that efficiency could get worse if consolidation goes too far. Thus, before taking action on particular courses, decisionmakers need to examine the potential reduced set of location candidates and compare them to the current distribution of training locations, students requiring training, training support costs, and expected training costs using a consolidated number of locations. In particular, we suggest verifying support cost savings, since the potential savings in training support manpower associated with superregional sites[6] is much less certain than the associated increase in travel cost.

Develop a Tracking System to Monitor Efficiency

To maintain and improve efficiency in the RC training system, decisionmakers must be able to measure it on an ongoing basis. Thus, we recommend that a tracking system be developed to monitor efficiency as the school system expands to other regions. It is important to note that we see this tracking system as an effective way to monitor the performance of the overall school system, but not as a way to compare the efficiency of individual schools.[7]

Because existing data systems do not supply all the required data in exactly the right format, RAND devised a number of data-collection instruments to fill in the

[4]This report does not address the potential for savings, especially in IDT, from increased use of distributed training methods.

[5]Our conclusions also support making resource information available to proponent schools so that their decisions can minimize costs while still training to standard.

[6]School manpower resourcing methods do not currently incorporate formal recognition of economies of scale in support manpower.

[7]In routinely tracking the efficiency of RC schools, commands need to realize that much of what drives efficiency (e.g., number of seats filled, match of actual course load with planned course load) is out of the schools' direct control. Thus, schools should primarily be evaluated based on their ability to implement training when planned student inputs equal actual student inputs and on their ability to respond to changes when actual student inputs deviate from what was originally planned.

gaps while conducting its two-year evaluation. We have drawn from those instruments to recommend a smaller set of data to be collected on an ongoing basis. (See the appendix for details.) Basically, the approach entails obtaining additional information from RC schools, command organizations, and instructors. At least some of the information could be routinely collected by adding a resource screen to the ATRRS system.

Refine TDAs and Make Them More Flexible

Further gains in efficiency will come from continuously reviewing the composition of school staffs for possible changes to reflect changes in requirements and forecasts of student inputs. Instructor needs should be derived from requirements, and TDAs should be "customized" for each school brigade and battalion in each region. Given the current uncertainties in estimating the demand for training to that level of detail, TDAs may require more frequent revision than they currently receive, reallocating personnel from areas of lesser need (e.g., common leader training) to areas of greater need (e.g., DMOSQ). Pursuing this strategy may also involve giving the schools more flexibility in making instructor substitutions when the balance of instructor needs suddenly changes.

Ensure That ADT/ADSW and TDY Resources Are Adequate to Support Changes in the Training System

Another way to ensure responsiveness and flexibility for schools, especially at a time when predictions of student load are uncertain, is to provide them with sufficient supplemental staff and instructor support resources to respond to ongoing changes in their environment. In the steady state, TDA instructor resources should be aimed at the low end of expected inputs, with temporary surges handled with ADSW resources. Further, during the transition period, at a time when the schools need to accommodate staff reductions from consolidation and need to organize to manage IDT over a much wider area,[8] extra resources for staff will be required to establish cost-effective work procedures[9] that will serve the schools in the long run.

---

[8]Our surveys of instructors have shown that the only area where training support in Region C was significantly worse than in Region E after one year of prototype implementation was in the area of DMOSQ IDT courses.

[9]For example, staff workload and support costs could be reduced if fewer and more permanent training sites were established.

Appendix

The Process of Tracking Resources and Costs

To improve efficiency in the RC training system, one must be able to measure it on an ongoing basis. Because existing data systems do not supply all the required data in exactly the right format, RAND devised a number of data-collection instruments to fill in the gaps while conducting its two-year evaluation. This appendix documents those instruments to support our recommendation that a tracking system be developed to monitor efficiency as the school system expands to other regions.

Calculating Student Days

Measuring efficiency requires calculating the number of student days and the number of school mandays—the numerator and denominator of our recommended measure of efficiency. "Student days" can be calculated using data extracted from ATRRS on inputs, graduates, date course beginning, and date course ending. The formula to compute student days is (graduates + inputs)/2 × course length in days. To calculate length of course for Phase I courses, we use the ATRRS course beginning and end dates and assume the course is run two days per month.[1] Alternatively, data on standard course length can be obtained from an external source.

Calculating School Mandays

Calculating "school mandays" of staff and instructors requires using a survey that we found was best filled out by RC school administrators. Existing data systems are insufficient because they merely track the total spent on assigned school manning. They do not yield the number of days bought for the money, nor do they provide any information about manpower borrowed from nonschool units (unless paid for by ADSW or ADT funds). Exhibit A.1 shows a survey design that captures the required information. The survey begins by asking about assigned military and civilian manpower, and then asks about lent and

---

[1] When employing this method, one must adjust for courses that contain both weekend and ADT training within one given time span (e.g., OCS). In those cases, course length must be individually calculated.

56

borrowed manpower by source of funding. Integrating the three pieces of data—adding assigned and borrowed and subtracting lent mandays—allows for total training manpower days for the school to be computed.[2] Finally, the survey contains questions designed to calculate days used for instructor and staff training and to determine the amount of unpaid time worked by school staff.

The survey uses a number of techniques to increase the accuracy of the response. First, in addition to asking for detailed information, the survey adds questions to allow estimates or approximations of answers when exact data are unavailable. Second, to allow cross-checking from one year to the next, the survey asks the respondent to compare data for the current year with data from the previous year. This helps identify disconnects in understanding that can occur with changeover in school personnel. Third, the survey shows how to ask questions to isolate specific issues of concern during a particular survey year. For example, the survey asks for specific estimates on the amount of manpower used in the process of borrowing equipment, a subset of total support manpower. Finally, one can use the RC schools administrative reports in conjunction with the survey of commands (described below) to ensure that personnel payments are consistent with the number of assigned days.

Determining Unreimbursed Travel Costs

Calculating unreimbursed travel costs is another issue. We developed a survey of instructors that included questions about unreimbursed expenses. The survey distinguishes between the costs of travel versus the costs for food and lodging and asks separate questions about travel for weekend training versus AT-mode training (see Exhibit A.2). This information should, if possible, be obtained at the AT itself, to include information from borrowed instructors.

Collecting O&M Costs

Collecting the O&M costs of a school can be useful to check on school manpower days (calculated in the RC schools survey, as described above) and to capture nonpersonnel costs, especially for brigades that intensively use expensive equipment. Some commands' financial systems allow them to pull off information about schools straightforwardly. Other commands find it necessary to obtain supplementary information from the school when the financial systems

---

[2]This survey technique can approximate total staff and instructor days at the battalion level of detail. Monitoring instructor days by MOS entails a supplementary effort that requires both financial and personnel information from the school and its command.

made it impossible to isolate school expenses or when a significant amount of training was funded from unit training dollars (without reimbursement). For this reason, we developed a survey to record the data (see Exhibit A.3).

Exhibit A.1

RCTI SURVEY DESIGN

FY _____ NUMBER OF SCHOOL STAFF IN TDA

Q1. Please indicate the total number of reserve component personnel assigned to (provisional or actual) TDA positions in your school during FY _____

Number of Personnel: _____

Q2. Please show the distribution of the total number of reserve component personnel listed in Q1 among the 10 staff categories listed below. Technicians should be listed twice—once in their civilian status, and again in their part-time military status.

STAFF CATEGORY		NUMBER OF PERSONNEL
Part-Time Military	Officer-Instructor	
	Officer-Staff	
	Enlisted-Instructor	
	Enlisted-Staff	
Full-Time Military	Officer-Instructor	
	Officer-Staff	
	Enlisted-Instructor	
	Enlisted-Staff	
Civilian	Technician	
	Other Civilian	

Q3. Please indicate the total number of active component personnel (i.e., Title XI) assigned to your school during FY _____.

Number of Personnel: _____

FY____ SCHOOL STAFF DAYS LENT

Q1. Considering as a group all courses taught by this institution in FY ____, which of the following statements best describes the percentage of **lent mandays** for instructors and staff. TDA staff are "lent" if they support courses not accredited to the school code(s) above, or if they perform work not associated with that school.

Instructors
- ❏ Less than 2 percent lent
- ❏ 2–9 percent lent
- ❏ 10–24 percent lent
- ❏ 25–49 percent lent
- ❏ 50 percent or more lent

Support Staff
- ❏ Less than 2 percent lent
- ❏ 2–9 percent lent
- ❏ 10–24 percent lent
- ❏ 25–49 percent lent
- ❏ 50 percent or more lent

Q2. Please provide a more precise answer to Q1 by estimating the number of days TDA school personnel were "lent" to other units during FY ___. Fill in the "total" column on the far right first; then, if the data is available, show the distribution by pay status in the other columns. If actual number of "lent" mandays is not known, please make an estimate.

STAFF CATEGORY		# IDT	# AT	#AGR	#ADT/ ADSW	TOTAL
Part-Time Military	Officer-Instructor					
	Officer-Staff					
	Enlisted-Instructor					
	Enlisted-Staff					
Full-Time Military	Officer-Instructor					
	Officer-Staff					
	Enlisted-Instructor					
	Enlisted-Staff					

Header: DAYS OF LENT SCHOOL STAFF TIME BY PAY STATUS

Q3. Compared to last year, the number of days TDA school personnel were lent to other units during FY___ (provided in Q2 above) was: *(Check One Box)*

- ❏ Much more (over 25 percent more)
- ❏ Somewhat more (5–25 percent more)
- ❏ About the same (less than 5 percent either way)
- ❏ Somewhat less (5–25 percent less)
- ❏ Much less (over 25 percent less)
- ❏ Don't know

60

FY___ SCHOOL STAFF DAYS BORROWED

Q1. Considering as a group all courses taught by this institution in FY___ which of the following statements best describes the percentage of **borrowed mandays** for instructors and staff? People are "borrowed" if they support courses accredited to the school code(s) listed above, but are assigned to another (school or nonschool) unit.

Instructors	Support Staff
❏ Less than 2 percent borrowed	❏ Less than 2 percent borrowed
❏ 2–9 percent borrowed	❏ 2–9 percent borrowed
❏ 10–24 percent borrowed	❏ 10–24 percent borrowed
❏ 25–49 percent borrowed	❏ 25–49 percent borrowed
❏ 50 percent or more borrowed	❏ 50 percent or more borrowed

Q2. Please provide a more precise answer to Q1 by estimating the actual number of mandays borrowed during FY___ to complete the school's mission. Fill in the "total" column on the far right first; then, if the data is available, show the distribution by pay status in the other columns. If the actual number of "borrowed" mandays is not known, please make an estimate.

STAFF CATEGORY AND SOURCE		# IDT	# AT	#AGR	#ADT/ ADSW	TOTAL
		DAYS OF BORROWED SCHOOL STAFF TIME BY PAY STATUS				
Borrowed From Other RCTI	Officer-Instructor					
	Officer-Staff					
	Enlisted-Instructor					
	Enlisted-Staff					
Borrowed From Non-School Units	Officer-Instructor					
	Officer-Staff					
	Enlisted-Instructor					
	Enlisted-Staff					

Q3. Compared to last year, the number of mandays borrowed from other units during FY___ (provided in Q2 above) was: *(Check One Box)*

❏ Much more (over 25 percent more)
❏ Somewhat more (5–25 percent more)
❏ About the same (less than 5 percent either way)
❏ Somewhat less (5–25 percent less)
❏ Much less (over 25 percent less)
❏ Don't know

PERSONNEL BORROWED FROM OTHER RESERVE COMPONENT(S)

Q4. Out of total mandays borrowed in Question 3 (previous page), estimate the number that were borrowed **FROM OTHER RESERVE OR ACTIVE COMPONENTS** to complete the school's mission. Include these only if not included in Question 2.

TYPE OF STAFF	Mandays Borrowed From Other RC or AC Components to Support FY____ School Mission	
	Officer	Enlisted
Instructors		
Support Staff		
Total		

ADT/ADSW FUNDS USED BY SCHOOL STAFF

Q6. Please estimate the number of mandays during FY___ where your own part-time staff worked additional periods in ADT/ADSW pay status to complete the school's mission.

STAFF CATEGORY		# ADT/ADSW (days)
Part-Time Military	Officer-Instructor	
	Officer-Staff	
	Enlisted-Instructor	
	Enlisted-Staff	

UNPAID TIME OF SCHOOL PERSONNEL

Q1. Estimate the number of UNPAID MANDAYS worked by school personnel (instructors or staff, organic or borrowed) in FY _____.

STAFF CATEGORIES	# of days
Instructors	
Support Staff	
Total	

Q2. Compared to last year, the amount of unpaid time in FY_____ (provided in Q1) was: *(Check One Box)*

❑ Much more (over 25 percent more)

❑ Somewhat more (5–25 percent more)

❑ About the same (less than 5 percent either way)

❑ Somewhat less (5–25 percent less)

❑ Much less (over 25 percent less)

❑ Don't know

COMMENTS ON TABLES 2.1–2.4: _____

_____

_____

_____

_____

_____

_____

FY_____ TRAINING OF SCHOOL STAFF

Q1. Estimate the number of mandays devoted to instructor and staff training during FY___. Include all DMOSQ, NCOES, refresher/proficiency, and instructor training courses taken by school staff.

Pay Status	FY___Total Days of Training	
	Instructor	Staff
IDT		
AT		
ADT/ADSW		
AGR (TDY)		
Other—Specify:		
Total		

Q2. Out of all mandays devoted to training of school staff in FY___ (enumerated in Q1 above), estimate the number that were **INSTRUCTOR TRAINING COURSES** (e.g., ITC, BFITC, SGITC, etc.).

Pay Status	FY___ Days of Training for Instructor Courses Only
IDT	
AT	
ADT/ADSW	
AGR (TDY)	
Other—Specify:	
Total	

SELECTED ACTIVITIES OF TRAINING MANPOWER

Q1. Estimate the mandays used by school personnel (instructors and staff, organic or borrowed) during FY___ on the process of borrowing equipment for IDT and AT training. Include both time spent coordinating the process prior to the class, and the time spent on transporting equipment during the course.

	IDT	AT
Number of days	_____	_____

Q2. Compared to last year, the amount of time spent on the borrowing of equipment in FY___ was: *(Check One Box)*

- ❏ Much more (over 25 percent more)
- ❏ Somewhat more (5–25 percent more)
- ❏ About the same (less than 5 percent either way)
- ❏ Somewhat less (5–25 percent less)
- ❏ Much less (over 25 percent less)
- ❏ Don't know

Q3. Estimate the mandays used by school personnel (instructors and staff, organic or borrowed) during FY___, if any, on these specialized training activities. Do not include support provided by installations.

	Number of days
Food service	_____
Medical support	_____

COMMENTS: _____

_____

_____

_____

_____

_____

Exhibit A.2

QUESTIONS FOR DETERMINING UNREIMBURSED TRAVEL COSTS FROM INSTRUCTOR SURVEY

AT/PHASE 2 TRAINING COURSE

1. How far is your residence from the AT/Phase 2 site?

   _____ Miles

2. How did you get to this AT/Phase 2 site?

   (Check One Box)
   ❏ POV
   ❏ Government Vehicle
   ❏ Military Aircraft
   ❏ Commercial Aircraft
   ❏ Other (specify)

3. Concerning this AT/Phase 2 course, did you incur (or do you expect to incur) expenses for hotel and food that will <u>not</u> be reimbursed? (Do not include any cost for miles.)

   (Check One Box)
   ❏ Yes ➔ Continue with Question 4
   ❏ No ➔ Go to Question 5, Next Page

4. Approximately, how much were (or do you expect will be) your expenses for hotel and food that will <u>not</u> be reimbursed for this AT/Phase 2 course? (Do not include the cost for miles.)

   (Check One Box)
   ❏ Less than $25
   ❏ $25–$49
   ❏ $50–$99
   ❏ $100–$199
   ❏ $200–$399
   ❏ $400 or more

5. Concerning this AT/Phase 2 course, did you incur (or do you expect to incur) mileage expenses that will <u>not</u> be reimbursed?

(Check One Box)

❏ Yes ➔ Continue with Question 6

❏ No ➔ Go to Question 7

6. Approximately, how much were (or do you expect will be) mileage expenses that will <u>not</u> be reimbursed for this AT/Phase 2 course? (Figure POV cost at $.30 per mile)

(Check One Box)

❏ Less than $25

❏ $25–$49

❏ $50–$99

❏ $100–$199

❏ $200 or more

IDT/PHASE 1 TRAINING COURSES

7. At how many locations did you teach IDT/Phase 1 courses during FY ____?

   NUMBER OF LOCATIONS: _____

8. For each location, list the number of round trips you made during FY ___ under Column A and the approximate distance from your home to the training site for this IDT/Phase 1 course under Column B.

	COLUMN A # of Round Trips	COLUMN B # of Miles From Home to IDT Site
Location 1	_____	_____
Location 2	_____	_____
Location 3	_____	_____

9. Did you receive (or do you expect to eventually receive) any TDY payments to cover any of your travel expenses to IDT training during the year for this course?

   (Check One Box)

   ❑ No   ❑ Yes ➜   Answer Question 10

10. How much TDY did you receive (or do you expect to receive) to cover all of FY__? If you don't know the exact amount, give us your best estimate using the ranges listed below.

    Amount $ _____ or estimate   ❑ Less than $50   ❑ $200–$299

    ❑ $50–$99   ❑ $300–$499

    ❑ $100–$199   ❑ $500 or more

11. Not including the cost of miles, did you incur (or do you expect to incur) significant food or hotel expenses in connection with IDT training for this course during the year for which there will be no reimbursement?

    (Check One Box)

    ❑ No   ❑ Yes ➜   Answer Question 12

12. How much were your unreimbursed travel expenses for this course? If you don't know the exact amount, give us your best estimate using the ranges listed below.

    Amount $ _____ or estimate   ❑ Less than $50   ❑ $200–$299

    ❑ $50–$99   ❑ $300–$499

    ❑ $100–$199   ❑ $500 or more

68

Exhibit A.3

COMMANDS SURVEY

SCHOOLS

Please list the names, school codes, and UICs of the school funded by this organization during FY__: Schools of interest include State Guard Academies, Regional NCO Academies, RFI Intelligence Schools, and RTS-Maintenance schools.

NO.	NAME	SCHOOL CODE(s)	UIC
1.	_____	_____	_____
2.	_____	_____	_____
3.	_____	_____	_____
4.	_____	_____	_____

TABLE 1

ESTIMATED FY___ PERSONNEL-RELATED EXPENDITURES IN SUPPORT OF SCHOOLS

POC Name for Table 1: _____

Commercial Phone: (   ) _____

Fill in the estimated personnel-related expenditures for each school under your jurisdiction.

(1)	(2)	(3)	(4)				(5)
			Cost ($) By School in FY ___				
Personnel Cost Category	MDEP Code(s)	AMSCO Code(s)	School Number ____	School Number ____	School Number ____	School Number ____	Total Cost for All Schools
a) Annual Training (AT)							
b) School Support (ADT/ADSW)							
c) Training of School Staff							
Other—list							
Other—list							

(1) *Cost Categories (rows):* The personnel cost categories in Table 1 can be directly related to Army Management Structure (AMS) codes used in Army accounting processes.

    a) "Annual training" expenditures come from "3A" accounts in the Army Reserve and "1A" accounts in the Army National Guard.

    b) "School support" is typically funded under "4G" accounts in the Army Reserve and "2F" accounts in the Army National Guard.

    c) "Training of School Staff" can be funded under "4F" accounts in the Army Reserve and "2F" accounts in the Army National Guard, but may also be funded under other accounts.

(2) *TDC code:* Management Decision Package code used in Army accounting processes.

(3) *AMSCO:* Army Management Structure Code used in Army Accounting processes.

(4) *School:* List the number from the first page of this report. Alternatively, use the ATRRS school code or school name or UIC.

(5) *Total:* Please provide a total cost, even if the total cannot be accurately related to specific schools.

If combined with expenses for full-time employees and IDT weekends of school staff, do you believe the above figures fairly represent the personnel-related cost of operating the above schools?

_____Yes (Go to next page)   _____ No (please explain below; attach extra sheet if necessary)

_____

_____

_____

_____

70

TABLE 2

ESTIMATED FY___ O&M AND OTHER EXPENDITURES IN SUPPORT OF SCHOOLS

POC Name for Table 2: _____

Commercial Phone: ( ) _____

(1)	(2)	(3)	(4)				(5)
			Amount ($) By School in FY___				
Cost Category	Object Class Code	AMSCO Code(s)	School Number ____	School Number ____	School Number ____	School Number ____	Total Cost for All Schools
Civilian pay	11–19						
TDY	21						
Supplies & materials: Total	26						
(SSSC)							
(POL)							
(Repair parts)							
(Other)							
Communications (e.g., phone)							
Postage							
Printing							
GSA leases							
Other contract svcs and splys	20 & 25						
Other leases (e.g., copier)	23						
Transportation of Things	22						
Ammunition							
Other training support— Attach a list							

(1) *Cost Categories (rows):*

TDY: refers to amounts for all unit personnel, both drilling soldiers and AGRs.

Supplies and Materials: include both the total for all supplies and materials, as well as the breakdowns for SSSC, POL, repair parts, and other supplies and materials.

Communications: Includes expenditures for phones, computer purchases and maintenance, copy supplies. Do not include the costs of postage and printing here, but rather in their separate categories below.

Postage and Printing: Please list approximate cost, regardless of who pays bill.

Other Contract Services and Supplies: For example, contracts for bus transportation, copier contract maintenance, KP contracts. If the total amount is significant, please break into components in an attachment.

Other leases: For example, other leased vehicles or leases of copy machines.

Transportation of Things: For example, transportation costs to move equipment to training site.

Ammunition: Please list approximate cost, regardless of who pays bill.

Other training support: For example, training aid maintenance, excess billeting costs, organizational clothing and equipment.

(2) *Object Class Code:* The "object class" code is part of the Standard Army Accounting Classification.

(3) *AMSCO:* Army Management Structure Code used in Army Accounting processes.

(4) *School Code:* List the number from the first page of this report. Alternatively, use the ATRRS school code or school name or UIC.

(5) *Total:* Please provide a total cost, even if the total cannot be accurately related to specific schools.

Aside from routine expenses for installation support (e.g., for utilities and real property maintenance), do you believe the above figures fairly represent the non-personnel-related cost of operating the above schools?

_____Yes   _____ No (please explain below; attach
                                                         extra sheet if necessary)

_____

_____

_____

_____

Bibliography

Department of the Army Inspector General (DAIG), *Special Assessment of Reserve Component Training*, Washington, D.C., January 11, 1993.

Orvis, Bruce R., Herbert J. Shukiar, Laurie L. McDonald, Michael G. Mattock, M. Rebecca Kilburn, and Michael G. Shanley, *Ensuring Personnel Readiness in the Army Reserve Components*, Santa Monica, CA: RAND, MR-659-A, 1995.

"Test Memorandum of Agreement (MOA) among the U.S. Army, the ARNG, and the USAR," June 24, 1993.

U.S. Army Training and Doctrine Command, *Training and Organization of the U.S. Army Reserve Components*, Fort Monroe, VA: U.S. Army Training Board, 1987.

————, *Concept Plan for Organizing a Total Army Training Structure (TATS) Individual Institutional Training System*, 1993.

————, *Cost Factor Handbook*, Fort Monroe, VA: 1995.

————, *Total Army School System OPLAN-1 (Future Army Schools 21st Century)*, U.S. Army Training and Doctrine Command, 1995.

Winkler, John D., Stephen J. Kirin, and John S. Uebersax, *Linking Future Training Concepts to Army Individual Training Programs*, Santa Monica, CA: RAND, R-4228-A, 1992.

Winkler, John D., et al., *Assessing the Performance of the Army Reserve Components School System*, Santa Monica, CA: RAND, MR-590-A, 1996.